Economic Analysis of Institutions and Systems

Svetozar Pejovich
Department of Economics,
Texas A&M University,
College Station, Texas

KLUWER ACADEMIC PUBLISHERS
DORDRECHT / BOSTON / LONDON

Library of Congress Cataloging-in-Publication Data

Pejovich, Svetozar.
Economic analysis of institutions and systems / by Svetozar Pejovich.
p. cm. -- (International studies in economics and econometrics)
Includes index.

1. Institutional economics. 2. Right of property. 3. Capitalism. 4. Socialism. I. Title. II. Series.
HB99.5.P45 1995
330--dc20 94-40239

DOI 10.1007/978-94-011-6483-2

Published by Kluwer Academic Publishers,
P.O. Box 17, 3300 AA Dordrecht, The Netherlands.

Kluwer Academic Publishers incorporates
the publishing programmes of
D. Reidel, Martinus Nijhoff, Dr W. Junk and MTP Press.

Printed on acid-free paper

ECONOMIC ANALYSIS OF INSTITUTIONS AND SYSTEMS

International Studies in Economics and Econometrics

VOLUME 33

The titles published in this series are listed at the end of this volume.

To my parents

TABLE OF CONTENTS

PREFACE

The cold-war years (1945-1989) had two interrelated effects on teaching and research in comparative economic systems. First, Economic systems were perceived a contest between capitalism and socialism. Second, teaching and research during cold war years emphasized macroeconomics, economic growth and all sorts of statistical comparisons between the United States and Western Europe on the one hand, and (mostly) the Soviet Union and Yugoslavia on the other.

In the late 1980s, East Europeans crossed the threshold of fear and forced their leaders to abandon both Marxism as a state religion and communism as a hazy vision of things to come. With the theory of history dead and buried, the cost of "building" socialism has increased relative to the present value of its expected future benefits. It is perhaps time to say: Economic Systems are Dead; Long Live Economic Systems.

The purpose of this book is to redirect study of what we used to call comparative economic systems toward analysis of the history and development of institutions, and the effects of alternative institutional arrangements on economic behavior. To this end, the book internalizes into a theoretical framework: (i) the effects of alternative institutions on the costs of transactions and incentive structures, (ii) the effects of the costs of transactions and incentives on economic behavior, and (iii) the evidence for refutable implications of those effects. In the process, it provides the logical premises for various institutions from which refutable implications can be deduced.

The book reveals my academic debt to a number of scholars, but especially to Armen Alchian, James Buchanan, Douglass North, and Richard Posner. I only hope that the book does not misrepresent (by much) their research.

Over a long period of time, the Earhart Foundation has supported my research, and, most importantly, helped me to formulate and stay on my own research-path. I couldn't have done it without the Foundation's support. I am also grateful to the Lynde and Harry Bradley Foundation for the financial support of my research on this book. An opportunity to spend several months at the International Centre for Economic Research in Turin, Italy gave me much needed time to plan this project.

I want to thank Enrico Colombatto from the University of Turin for his support and encouragement in writing this book, Angelo Petroni from the University of Bologna for teaching me that economists could gain a lot from listening to philosophers of science, and to my dear friend Joze Mencinger from the University of Ljubljana for so many useful discussions during our long walks and even longer dinners in Turin. Special thanks to John Moore from George Mason University for inviting me to several conferences dealing with issues important to this book.

Sally Antrobus provided valuable editorial assistance, Susan Dederich-Pejovich, my wife, provided "on-site" technical support for my computer, and my whole family let me work in peace, while giving loving support and understanding.

Svetozar Pejovich
College Station, Texas
Summer 1994

PART ONE

INSTITUTIONS AND PROPERTY RIGHTS

Chapter 1

THE NATURE OF ECONOMICS

THE ROOTS OF ECONOMIC PROBLEMS

We all have unsatisfied wants. Just ask yourself if there is something that you would like to have but have not been able to afford? You can also ask your parents, friends and even strangers. They will all agree that they have unsatisfied wants. Some of us may think that the very rich have everything. But we cannot be sure they have everything *they* want. In fact they would tell you that there are many things they want but have to do without. The message is quite simple. On the issues of aspirations, tastes, preferences, desires and feelings, we can only speak for ourselves. And speaking for ourselves, we all have unsatisfied wants.

The fact that we all have unsatisfied wants means that we live in a world of scarcity. Scarcity means that in order to get a little bit more of any good, a little bit of other goods has to be given up. Regardless of how much money I have, every time I spend five dollars on a pastrami sandwich, I give up satisfaction from another bundle of goods that five dollars could buy. A student deciding to study on a Saturday night gives up the satisfaction of going out on a date. No matter how affluent or poor we are as individuals or as a nation, scarcity is always present; that is, what we want exceeds what is available. *In a world of scarcity an increment in satisfaction from any good has its cost: the value of that which is being given up.*

The desire for more utility (satisfaction) is a behavioral consequence of the fact that we all have unsatisfied wants. It predicts our behavior in a world in which what people want exceeds what they have. The attitude that more satisfaction is preferred to less satisfaction might have helped humanity to survive competition from other forms of life. We generalize this behavior as our search for more utility.

All of human history is about our search for more utility. Individuals demand only those goods that give them utility or satisfaction. Anything that yields satisfaction to someone is then a good. It could be a physical object (a crystal vase), something to eat (ice cream), an activity (dating), or doing things for others (contributing to boy scouts). A greedy, rational, calculating "economic man" exists only in some obsolete books. In the real world, individuals have diverse preferences, aspirations and values. They go on, day in and day out, learning about alternatives, interpreting them, and choosing those which they expect to make them better off.

THE PROBLEM OF CHOICE

We satisfy wants by acquiring goods. But goods have to be produced. To produce goods we need to use a multitude of things including land, machines, people, raw materials, "gifts" of nature, and time (e.g., to develop a friendship). All those things become resources when we develop a desire for the goods they help to produce (e.g., oil had been known to American Indians for a long time before it became a resource). It is probably correct to say that resources are created rather than found.

In addition to being scarce, resources have alternative uses. I can either work for government or teach, but I cannot do both at the same time. You can always grow a little bit more food in your yard at the cost of having less grass. A student could choose to study longer for a test in economics at the cost of giving up a bit of other activities that are also demanded; a building could be used as a factory or residence; and so on. The point is that whenever we use resources to produce a little more of something we, in effect, choose to produce less of something else. Next time your senator tells you that the state needs another highway, ask what it is that the taxpayers can do without.

Every time people decide to buy something, they have less income left for other things; and each time they choose to engage in an activity, they have less time for other activities. When a community decides to produce a few more cigars, it must give up something else that the same bundle of resources (land, machines, people, etc.) could have produced. We could get slightly cleaner air at a cost of reducing the supply of other goods (e.g. cars). A key proposition then is that we can identify the cost of any bundle of goods in terms of alternative bundles.

The fact of scarcity helps us to understand the nature of human choices. Most human decisions are marginal (more or less of A in exchange for less or more of other things) rather than total (all or nothing of A). For example, from the standpoint of individual members of a community, the relevant criterion in making their choices on protection from crime, certainly a useful good, is the relationship between the incremental benefits from a little less crime and the incremental costs in terms of other things that have to be sacrificed. The issue is not one of crime or no crime.

Economics is thus the science of choice. It analyses human behavior with respect to social issues arising from the fact of scarcity. Moreover, economics is a positive science. It does not judge human actions as good or bad, rational or irrational, desirable or undesirable. Economic analysis merely seeks to identify circumstances that affect the costs of alternative choices, to analyze their implications for human decisions, and to make verifiable predictions about economic outcome. Economics is about logic and empirical evidence.

An implication is that facts and observations mean little by themselves. They become useful only in the context of a theory. Economic theories are generalized propositions of cause and effect. Economic theories have to be general, that is, capable of explaining a wide class of real world events, and relevant, that is, capable of yielding observable propositions.

Given that resources are scarce relative to human wants and are capable of alternative uses, all human societies have to resolve two fundamental survival issues: *who gets what* and *who does what*. The former is about the distribution of goods that have already been produced. Each time an individual gets a bit of something, that much less is left for others. The latter is about production. Every time we assign a resource to produce something, we are giving up a bundle of other things the same resource could have produced.

Those two fundamental issues have their origin in scarcity. However, solutions to who gets what and who does what depend on prevailing institutional arrangements.

Economic analysis of institutions does not require references to capitalism and socialism. However, the convention of referring to those two systems is both strong and useful. The history and development of capitalism and socialism help us understand the forces that contributed to the rise of many institutions. And categorizing some institutions as having the characteristics of capitalism or socialism reduces the cost of identifying their intended consequences.

Chapter 2

THE RISE OF CAPITALISM AND SOCIALISM

How did various institutions emerge? Are they unintended consequences of the gradual evolution of human knowledge and technology or intended consequences of social engineering? Are they predictable outcomes of the laws of history? A review of the history and development of capitalism and socialism addresses a number of those issues.

THE MIDDLE AGES

The collapse of the Roman Empire eliminated both Roman law, which was based on private ownership and contracts, and the machinery that enforced it. Initially, barbaric customs replaced Roman law as the means of resolving conflicts of interest among competing individuals and groups.

A survival strategy for a weaker man was to turn to a stronger man and give the latter nontransferable right of ownership in his land in exchange for protection and an inalienable right of tenancy--the right to hold the land of the lord. The lord-vassal relationship slowly evolved into a basic social institution in medieval Europe. The land held by the vassal was called the feud. A lord could and often did become the vassal of still another man; that is, he became both the lord of a weaker man and the vassal of a stronger man. Eventually, the high costs of negotiating, policing and enforcing one's rights to life and property in post-Roman Europe gradually led to the development of a socioeconomic system based on a hierarchy of individuals holding specific property rights in land. The king was at the top of this chain of pseudo-contractual relationships, and the actual tillers of the land (serfs) were at the bottom.

The Catholic Church was the most powerful institution in the Middle Ages. The church had no opposition in matters of faith. In a well-researched book on the Middle Ages, William Manchester wrote:

> Saint Augustine (354-430) devoted thirteen years to writing De Civitates Dei (The City of God), the first great work to shape and define the medieval mind....He divided all creation into civitas Dei and civitas terrena. Everyone had to embrace one of them, and a man's choice would determine where he spent eternity....Because he had identified the Church with his civitas Dei, Augustine clearly implied the need for a theocracy, a state in which secular power, symbolizing civitas terrena, would be subordinate to spiritual powers derived from God. The Church, drawing the inference, thereafter used Augustine's reasoning as an ideological tool and, ultimately, as a weapon in grappling with kings and emperors....the entire medieval millennium took on the aspect of triumphant Christendom. As aristocracies arose from the barbaric mire, kings and princes owed their legitimacy to divine authority, and squires became knights by praying all night at Christian altars. Sovereigns courting popularity led crusades to the Holy Land. To eat meat during Lent became a capital offense, sacrilege meant imprisonment, the Church became the wealthiest landowner on the Continent, and the life of every European, from baptism through matrimony to burial, was governed by popes, cardinals...The clergy, it was believed, would cast decisive votes in determining where each soul would spend the afterlife.[1]

The Catholic Church also acquired a substantial monopoly in the field of education. Libraries were located in monasteries and cathedrals, and the vast majority of literate people were monks. By being the repository of accumulated knowledge, the church had the power to

---

[1] Manchester, W. A World Lit Only By Fire, Boston: Little, Brown and Company, 1993, pp. 9-11.

interpret knowledge, to determine its uses, and to influence the direction of its growth.

The power of the church explains two important features of community life in the Middle Ages: (i) a strong marriage between theology and philosophy, and (ii) an equally strong marriage between ethics and economics. The laws, customs, and social institutions of the Middle Ages were either determined or approved by the church. Religious life and everyday social life were largely indistinguishable in the Middle Ages.

By the end of the ninth century, this synthesis of religion and secular life took the form of a feudal society with a distinct and sharply defined class structure. Mobility between social classes was limited. A child born to a peasant would remain a peasant for life. A child born to a noble family became a member of the nobility. Every person was entitled to the means of subsistence suited to his or her station in life.

The role of philosophy was to explain and support theological conclusions. Any conflict between the two was considered to be caused by some philosophical error. Thus, philosophy in the Middle Ages was largely a handmaiden to theology. Similarly, economic activities in the Middle Ages were regulated by ethical criteria. The legitimacy of economic activities was tested by reference to moral teachings of the church, not to utility.

The medieval church was thus the final authority in morality, social life, and economic activity. It provided the philosophical rationale, the moral justification, and the religious sanction for the socioeconomic system which had emerged more or less spontaneously. The moral basis for the political authority and socioeconomic privileges of medieval nobility was said to be divine right. That is, kings and lords ruled by the grace of God rather than with the consent of their subjects. Secular rulers in the Middle Ages, then, needed the church on their side.

The church recognized the necessity of trade but warned that such economic activity stimulated the acquisitive spirit, which was perilous to the soul. Hence it is not surprising that trade was dominated by Jews, who lived outside the Christian orbit. The spirit of acquisition and the accumulation of wealth were condemned by the church. The high watermark of the attack on the spirit of acquisition was reached in the thirteenth century. Thomas Aquinas and his followers, called the schoolmen, set down explicit rules regarding economic activities in general and the concept of "just" price in particular. According to the schoolmen, the just price of any good was to be equal to its cost of production plus a margin required to sustain the seller's customary standard of living, and no more than that. Money was considered a nonproductive medium of exchange, and it was wrong to charge interest on borrowed funds.

The universe was assumed to be static and preordained. People had set places in society with obligations and privileges prescribed for their stations in life. The only purpose of knowledge was to help people understand God's intentions in creating the universe.

THE GREAT TRANSFORMATION

For fourteen centuries after the death of Jesus, the church was all-powerful, the afterlife was a certainty, and all knowledge was known. The established order was strong and resistant to social change. It would have been impossible for a single factor to bring about its demise. This section will describe some of the factors that played a role in the great transformation from feudalism to capitalism.

Philosophical Factors

The fifteenth century witnessed the emergence of educated classes inflamed by anticlericalism, inspired in part by corruption within the church. Another important source of anticlericalism was revival of interest in the cultural heritage of Rome and Greece, with emphasis on law and reason respectively. Powerful new ideas, subversive of all that medieval society had stood for, were spontaneously emerging in Europe. As William Manchester observes:

> The mighty storm was swiftly approaching, but Europeans were not aware of it....Shackled in ignorance, disciplined by fear, and sheathed in superstition, they trudged into the sixteenth century...their vacant faces, pocked by smallpox, turned blindly toward the future they thought they knew.[1]

The process of alienation of philosophy from theology started with nominalism in the fourteenth century. Nominalists such as the English philosopher William Occam declared that the gulf between reason and theology was real and unbridgeable. The idea of the separation of philosophy from theology gained momentum with the development of the scientific method of looking at the world. Francis Bacon (1561-1626), John Locke (1632-1704) and David Hume (1711-1776), among others, raised the issue of the supremacy of reason and knowledge over the revealed truth. Their method of analysis was experimentation and the objective was to enhance knowledge. Bacon argued for the progress of science and its application to human life. Locke thought that the state should support natural laws and that within this structure the individual should have free rein. Hume argued for private property rights.

On the continent, Rene Descartes (1596-1650), Isaac Newton (1642-1727) and August Comte (1798-1857), again among others, emphasized the importance of mathematics and science. Descartes claimed that mathematics could be extended to philosophy. Newton was concerned with the rules of reasoning in philosophy. Comte argued that actual knowledge depends on testing. Immanuel Kant (1724-1804), a leading rationalist in the eighteenth century, insisted on the authority of science.

These philosophical developments in Europe were the result of a desire to improve understanding of the world by emphasizing reason, science and experimentation. The alienation of philosophy from theology was applied to economic life by Adam Smith, whose

---

[1] Manchester, W. A World Lit Only By Fire, p. 27.

Wealth of Nations marked the beginning of economics as a social science.

The Religious Reformation

In The Protestant Ethics and the Spirit of Capitalism, Max Weber offered an extensive analysis of the role of reformation on the spiritual and material life of medieval man. The purpose of Weber's analysis was to establish the sources from which modern man derived his principles. He thought that the new social order was a consequence of the triumph of the acquisitive instinct. And this triumph became possible through the growing acceptance of the concept of *calling*, especially in its Calvinistic expression.

To Martin Luther (1483-1546), calling meant the state of life in which the individual has been set by heaven, and against which it was impious to rebel. Each person, according to Luther, was given a station in life by God and was expected to become successful in a calling--but within the limits established for that station by the medieval social structure.

To John Calvin (1509-1564), calling was an enterprise that an individual chooses with a sense of religious responsibility. Calvin, who picked up Luther's concept of calling, defended the moral justification of worldly activities and added to it his teaching of the predestination of man. Calvin thought that by God's will some people are predestined for salvation, others for damnation. An individual's material success is the sign of being among those chosen for salvation. To prove themselves among the chosen, individuals have to work hard and live frugally.

Calvin taught that people are free to choose their own calling. But once the choice is made, they must do everything within their physical and intellectual powers to prove themselves successful. Thus, Calvin justified, on religious grounds, the accumulation of wealth. The Puritan spirit that emerged from Calvin's teaching gave tremendous impetus to the development of the frugal, hard-working and accumulating individual. It is interesting to note that capitalism first developed in two countries with Puritan populations: England and Holland. It was also more successful in protestant North America than in catholic South America.

New Frontiers

New philosophy gave birth to new ideas. However, tradition in Europe was strong. The old order, with its customs, class privileges, and medieval values, was powerful and resistant to new ideas. Traditional Christianity was too deeply rooted in people's minds to be quickly altered. Moreover, Europe was poor and too overcrowded to offer "room" for new ideas to be given an empirical test. New concepts lacked the space to be tried out. The exploration and settlement of new frontiers, primarily in North America, provided an excellent laboratory for new ideas.

The most important contribution of new frontiers to the great transformation of medieval society into the world we know was in providing a tradition-free space in which to test new ideas. Freedom from religious constraints, from humble origins, and from traditional ethics allowed thousands of people to pursue their individual preferences, to take responsibility for their own actions, and to create their own way of life. Once those ideas were applied to everyday life and proven successful, they traveled back to Europe and contributed substantially there to the transformation of the medieval world into the modern society.

The people who went to North America in the early days of the new frontiers were often referred to as criminal elements. Indeed, they were criminals by the then prevailing standards, when it was a crime to oppose the established order, reject medieval tradition, complain about the church, and avoid taxes imposed by kings, feudal lords and bishops. Most settlers came to America to escape those restrictions. They had a "rebellious" desire to make their own choices, choose their own morals, and develop their own rules of the game.

Besides providing a tradition-free space for the application of new ideas, the new frontiers made an additional contribution to the great transformation. Of every $100 worth of gold and silver produced in Western Europe and the New World after 1492, $85 worth was produced in the new frontiers. Taking precious metals and other goods to Europe was quite risky but also quite profitable. Thus, the activity happened. An unintended result of this individual risk-taking was to give new ideas a chance to demonstrate their social and economic consequences.

Sociological Factors

The great transformation required a middle class, a supply of labor, and a positive attitude toward work--none of which existed, in an institutional sense, in the Middle Ages.

Medieval nobility could not supply entrepreneurship. Its concerns were wars, politics, and leisure. It was degrading for a nobleman to engage in commercial activities, trade and crafts. He was born to be a lord, a hunter, a lover, and a warrior. Entrepreneurship emerged from the ranks of small traders and artisans. Those people were envious of all the status, privileges, and wealth enjoyed by the nobility. They also wanted to draw a line between themselves and the lower class of peasants. In the quest for status and influence, small traders and artisans turned their energies toward the accumulation of wealth. Eventually, they laid out the foundation for the emergence of an entrepreneurial class.

The labor force emerged from several sources. The rate of population growth in Europe in the aftermath of the Black Death (fourteenth century) was an important factor. With an increase in the population, the marginal productivity of serfs fell relative to the value of land. This change in the economic conditions of life provided incentives for the land-owning aristocracy to seek to replace the feudal system of nontransferable ownership that tied peasants to their land with private, transferable ownership of land. Enclosures and other methods of throwing peasants off the land were an important source of labor. Among other factors that led to an increase in the supply of labor were improvements in health care, the gradual disappearance of private armies and guilds, and the advent of child labor.

In the scheme of social values that prevailed in the Middle Ages, begging and physical labor were considered two acceptable methods of survival for the poor. The religious reformation was largely responsible for developing a positive attitude toward work. By giving strong religious sanctions to hard work, the Reformation divorced productive work from welfare. A person's attitude toward work became a measure of character and integrity.

Capital Formation.

On the supply side, two major sources of investable funds are private savings and bank credit. Neither existed in the Middle Ages. Private wealth was spent on the church, palaces, private armies, luxuries, purchasing insurance policies (e.g., building cathedrals), and many other activities, or was reserved for heirs.

The Reformation had strong influence on the supply of private savings. To prove themselves chosen for salvation and to avoid temptations, people had to work hard and live frugally. This religious sanction for the accumulation of wealth opened the door for private savings.

Medieval banks did not give credit. Their major function was to safeguard deposits and transfer them from one account to another. According to Joseph Schumpeter, the failure of medieval banks to create bank credit was a major reason that Italian cities such as Florence, Genoa and Venice were not able to sustain their prosperity. The development of the modern banking system began in 1694, when the Bank of England was founded. It gained momentum in 1797, when the British government forbade the bank to pay its notes in gold, opening the door to a rapid increase in the volume of bank credit. When the gold standard was reimposed in 1821, the ability of banks to create credit, a vital source of capital formation, was firmly established.

THE RISE OF CAPITALISM

Capitalism emerged via coalescence of many factors, most of which were not new. Reason had played an important role in classical Greece; the tradition of law had been a cornerstone of the social order in Rome; and the benefits of free trade had long been appreciated in the Middle East. Adam Smith described the system, which he called the Natural System of Economic Liberty, as being self-generating, self-propelling, and self-regulating. Some people called it laissez-faire. Property rights scholars refer to the system as the private-property, free-market economy. Marxists and pro-Marxists named the system capitalism with a tone of ethical and social disapproval. And the name they gave to the system prevailed.

Whatever we choose to call it, the system that slowly replaced feudalism was an unintended consequence of many factors that occurred almost simultaneously starting in the fifteenth century. Its cornerstones were classical liberal philosophy and methodological individualism. The former is about individual liberty, openness to new ideas, tolerance of all views, and the rule of law. The latter says that the individual is the only decision maker. That is, to understand decisions made by entities such as governments, corporations and other types of organizations, it is necessary to recognize decision makers in those organizations, pay attention to their private ends, and identify the incentives under which they work.

The capitalist community can then be defined as a voluntary association of individuals who join and leave the group in the pursuit of their own private ends. Capitalism emphasizes the rights of the individual over those of the group, and assumes behavior to be based on self-interest, self determination, self-responsibility and market competition.

THE CRITICS OF CAPITALISM

Catholic theologians and socialists were the most serious critics of early capitalism. Both these categories of thinkers believed that the community has a system of desired outcomes, and that the rules of the game must be designed to channel individual behavior toward those common objectives.

Early Catholic Philosophy

Early Catholic theologians and philosophers raised the issue of the legitimacy of capitalism as a moral system. Judging by the content of a number of recent announcements from Vatican, the conservative wing of the Catholic Church still has misgivings about capitalism. Goetz Briefs, a distinguished catholic philosopher and economist wrote:

> The 16th and 17th centuries were the age of discoveries and the struggle for colonial possessions....Soldiers, merchants and traders overran a pagan, alien and assumedly savage world--a world where Christian community ethics did not apply. Consequently what came to be applied was a commercial self-interest on a purely competitive scale. A pragmatic "alien ethos"--ethics ruling relationships between mutual aliens--was adopted with no holds barred. Compared with Christian standards it was definitely submarginal, but in political and commercial terms it proved to be eminently successful. This alien ethos, originally formed outside the Christian orbit, gradually came to be accepted among traders and businessmen--first in the metropolises of colonial ventures and enterprise, in Holland and England. No wonder that some Dutch and English traders, financiers and merchants were the first openly to extol the blessings of uninhibited trade, of self-interest and competition.[1]

The origin of catholic philosophers' unease with the system lies in the basic difference between the Catholic and the capitalist concepts of

---

[1] Briefs, G., "The Ethos Problem in the Present Pluralistic Society," Review of Social Economy, 15, 1957, p. 51.

the community. What a classical liberal considers as the freeing of individuals from the constraints of (medieval) tradition, a conservative Catholic philosopher sees as erosion of morality and rejection of "absolute" values. Conservative Catholic philosophy is apprehensive about freedom of choice not because of any lack of interest in individual liberty, but because of a fear that autonomy of individual choices in the free market does not necessarily generate morally satisfying sets of preferences. It ignores the fact that the free market does not generate preferences. Those who are critical of the freedom of individual choice should direct their criticism toward the institutions--such as schools, churches, the streets, households, the media--that participate in the formation of our preferences, rather than toward the free market in which those preferences are merely revealed. Suppressing freedom of choice does not change a person's character. It merely deprives people of an opportunity to choose and bear the cost of a choice (e.g., losing friends). While the free market does not make people moral, it raises the cost of unethical behavior. In 1920s, Ludwig von Mises addressed the issue of the relationship between the church and capitalism as follows:

> It would be foolish to maintain that Enlightenment, by undermining the religious feelings of the masses, had cleared the way for socialism. On the contrary, it is the resistance which the Church offered to the spread of liberal ideas which has prepared the soil for ...modern socialist thought....Christian socialism has done hardly less than atheist socialism to bring about the present state of confusion.[1]

Early (Pre-Marx) Socialists

Sir Thomas More (1478-1535) was the first significant critic of capitalism. In his writing, More tried to tie socialist ideas to the moral teachings of the early church fathers.

---

[1] Mises, L. Socialism, Indianapolis: Liberty Fund. Inc., pp. 379-81.

More opposed the transformation of the traditional society into a money economy. He realized that the world was changing but argued that changes must be made within the bounds of the moral teachings of the church. On a practical level, More believed in primitive communism. Medieval philosophers and early socialists defined primitive communism as a society in which all resources are held in common and no member of the community is allowed to accumulate private wealth. By establishing common ownership of all resources, More believed, the problems of the emerging industrial society could be resolved or avoided. More also believed that private property rights make a just government impossible. Private property rights, he claimed, lead to social inequalities, which generate behaviors that are contrary to divine law.

More's alternative to the emerging capitalist society was the concept of utopia. In utopia, agriculture was the most important industry. All citizens, including those living in the cities, must spend some time working on collective farms. The supply of goods for all cities is to be calculated in advance, and their citizens have to work on the farms in proportion to their cities' food needs. Every month a member of each family would be required to take goods produced by the family to the market. In exchange, the family would receive coupons which it would exchange for other goods in the market. To travel from one community to another would require permission. And the traveler would have to do a day's work at the destination.

In the seventeenth and eighteenth centuries, France became fertile ground for socialist ideas. Unlike Thomas More, who wanted to retreat from capitalism and return to the customs and morality of the old order, French socialists accepted the reality of the rising industrial society and raised a question: What can be done to eliminate the social and economic inequalities of capitalism?

Comte Henri de Saint Simon (1760-1825) and Pierre Joseph Proudhon (1809-1865) were the most prominent among French socialists. Saint Simon participated in the American Revolution and was decorated for bravery during the battle of Yorktown. His primary objective was to find a way to guarantee equal opportunity rather than economic equality. And Saint Simon believed that the only way to achieve equal opportunity was through collective ownership. As a result of his conclusion, he directed his major criticism of capitalism at private property rights. Long before Marx, Saint Simon advocated "from each according to his ability; to each according to his contribution." Like all other socialists, Proudhon opposed private property rights. But, unlike Saint Simon, he believed in actual economic equality.

Robert Owen (1771-1858) is usually called the father of British socialism. Like most early socialists, Owen blamed private property rights for unemployment, child labor, poverty and poor working conditions. He believed that the primary objective of human existence is to be happy but, he claimed, happiness cannot be obtained individually. In fact, he argued that competition and individualism lead to the degradation of labor. The remedy he proposed was communism, which would prohibit private property rights.

What was the common denominator in the ideas of early socialist thinkers? They all believed that a happy and harmonious community is possible. However, they saw private property rights as destroying this natural harmony and, as a consequence, preventing the happiness of the individual. They saw *human reason* as a vehicle for rediscovering the world of peace and harmony. Harry Laidler, a student of socialism, wrote in 1927:

> Social change was regarded by [early socialists] as largely a result of the social discovery of brilliant men. If some one in society five hundred years before their time had discovered the truth which they were proclaiming, and had explained these truth to their fellowmen, misery and suffering, they felt, would long since have disappeared. For absolute truth is independent of time, space...and it is thus a mere accident when and where it is discovered. [Early socialists] also had the mistaken notion that it was possible for social thinkers to cut out a pattern of a future order in all of its details, and that

mankind could be induced to follow faithfully every detail of that pattern.[1]

Marxism

Karl Marx (1818-1883) was born in the Rhineland of Germany. He was one of seven children in a Jewish family that embraced Christianity when he was six years of age. Marx studied philosophy, history, law and literature in Bonn and Berlin. Eventually, he became the most influential critic of capitalism. He was a prolific writer whose contributions cannot be easily summarized in a few pages. This section will briefly review the sources of influence on Marx and the process of social change as he saw it.

The Sources of Influence on Marx. Marx was influenced by three contemporary movements: early (French) socialism, classical German philosophy, and classical British economics.

French socialists believed that capitalism was an immoral system. They blamed capitalism for long working hours, child labor, the poverty of working people, unemployment, income inequalities, social injustice, and other problems. And they placed the ultimate blame for these problems on private property rights. Thus, French socialists argued that the simplest way to do away with capitalism and the ills to which it seemed tied to was to abolish private property rights.

Marx agreed with French socialists that capitalism was not a just system. He also agreed with their criticism of private property rights. However, Marx considered it naive to think that socialism, once discovered by reason, could conquer the world simply by promising justice and harmony. He drew a line between the preference for socialism and the scientific analysis of its role in

---

[1] Laidler, H. A History of Socialist Thought, New York: Thomas Crowell Co. 1927, p. 139.

human history. The fallacy of reason, Marx believed, is that it ignores the laws of history; ideas have to await their moments in history.

The great thinkers of the Middle Ages considered the universe as constant and eternal. Eventually, scholars began to realize that human history is an endless evolution of social institutions. This discovery that the universe is not immutable generated interest in the process of social change. G.W.Friedrich Hegel (1770-1831) was a leading philosopher among those who tried to formulate a theory of social change. His central thesis was that prevailing ideas determine our perceptions about the world in which we live. These common ideas shape our social institutions, the way we interact with each other, and the organization of production and distribution of goods. The essence of Hegel's philosophical method was the concept of dialectics: Each idea has its internal contradiction, and within each idea there is a conflict between its positive and negative elements. It is from this internal conflict inherent in all ideas that a new idea eventually emerges. This new idea is not an extension of the old one. Being a qualitatively different concept, the new idea slowly but surely reshapes all aspects of social life.

Marx accepted Hegel's thesis that human history is shaped by social changes generated from within the social system itself. However, he disagreed with Hegel as to the role of ideas in producing social changes. Marx asserted that the economic conditions of life determine our social institutions, politics, philosophy, religion and ideas. That is, Marx moved Hegel's concept of progress from the sphere of ideas to the material world. Quite appropriately, Marx's method of analysis is called *dialectical materialism*. It says that the process of social change, which occurs through a struggle of positive and negative elements within the prevailing system, consists of the gradual accumulation of small quantitative changes that lead to a major qualitative change in the system. For example, private property rights is the positive element in capitalism, while the proletariat is its negative element (i.e., internal contradiction). In the "dialectical" struggle between private property rights and the rising proletariat, the latter has to triumph. Socialism, a qualitatively different system, will then replace capitalism by abolishing both the proletariat and private property rights.

Marx was also influenced by David Ricardo (1770-1823), from whom he borrowed the labor theory of value. This theory basically said that the value of any commodity is proportional to the average number of labor hours needed for its production. Thus, only labor creates new value; the contribution of capital to the value of a product is equal to its wear and tear. For example, under the labor theory of value, a serving of beer would be worth twice as much as a soft drink if its production required twice as many labor hours.

Marx modified the labor theory of value to suit his purpose. He said that if the value of any good is determined by the average number of hours needed for its production, the value of labor must also be determined by the average number of hours needed for its production. Each day workers use up a certain amount of their energy, which must be replenished so that they are able to work the next day. They must also be able to support their children who will eventually replace them in the labor force. The market wage, then, is the amount of money that is just sufficient to buy the minimum bundle of goods needed for a worker's maintenance. The value of this bundle of goods is the average number of labor hours needed to produce it.

Suppose the working day is ten hours, but that it takes only five hours to produce the minimum bundle of goods a worker must receive each day. In ten hours, that worker creates the value that brings the employer (i.e., the property owner) an amount of money equal to ten labor-hours. The employer pays the worker a wage that is equal to the value of five labor-hours. The difference between the number of hours the worker labors each day and the number of hours it takes to produce the minimum bundle of goods that worker must have each day is the *surplus value*. The surplus value is captured by the class of property owners.

The Process of Social Change. Marx believed that economic processes explain all of human history, which he saw as a continuous struggle against nature. Triggered by our survival instinct (we would say today by our desire for utility), the ultimate purpose of this struggle is to reverse the original relationship between human beings and nature.

The sequence begins with primitive society. There, people were totally dependent for their economic survival on an alien and hostile environment. All efforts in a primitive society were geared toward the restricted objective of subsistence, that is, toward the appropriation of products in their natural state. Without innovation, primitive society would have merely reproduce itself through time. However, the survival instinct led people to seek ways to produce subsistence more efficiently, The discovery of fire made fish an important source of nourishment, the bow and arrow increased returns from hunting, etc. As people learned how to use intermediate goods (tools) to increase the supply of food for subsistence, two related developments had to occur.

First, each time a person creates a new tool (primitive hammer or modern computer), humanity takes a step toward freedom from dependence on nature. Human history, then, is a long journey from our complete economic subordination to nature to our ultimate mastery over nature, in his view. This last stage in our journey through history Marx called communism. In today's jargon, Marx's communism could be called a world without scarcity. At any rate, the economic interpretation of history has a strong pseudo-religious content: salvation will happen in this space and time.

Second, as people learned to produce and use tools, it became necessary for them to regulate access to those tools. To define who has what access to an asset means to define property rights in that asset. Thus, Marx had a theory of the spontaneous development of property rights. He deduced the development of property rights from the initial human alienation from nature, and our (survival) instinct to reverse that relationship. Property rights did not develop because a few "wise" souls discovered their importance.

While the importance of property rights had been recognized by scholars before him, Marx was the first to have a theory of property rights. His analytical apparatus was primitive and his deterministic views of human history untenable. Yet, Marx was able to perceive the importance of property rights for the allocation and use of scarce resources, to recognize that property rights are endogenous to the system, and to sense that property relations have specific and predictable effects on human behavior.

Marx used two general concepts to explain the process of social change leading to the final stage of communism: (i) The productive forces represent the relation between people and nature in the production of goods and services. Marx included in this concept technology, the supply of resources, the work ethic, and education. and the relations of production or property relations. (ii) The relations of production or property relations are the relations among people in the process of production. Today, we would probably call these a social system. Throughout human history, the relations of production are relations among aliens. Marx's analysis of the concept of alienated labor, one of his key concepts, explains this point.

1. Since it does not belong to him or her, the product of a worker's labor appears to that worker to be an alien object.

2. Consequently, the worker considers his work to be imposed labor, and is thus alienated from the work activity.

3. What distinguishes people from animals is our consciousness and self-awareness as regards our life-activity, including work. But alienated labor turns a key life activity into a mere means of subsistence, thus alienating people from their species life.

4. The worker is alienated from that the owner of the means of production, who owns the product of that worker's labor.

5. Workers and owners, alienated from each other, belong to identifiable social classes. The class struggle is thus a major consequence of private property rights.

How does the process of social change work? In its journey through history, humans must pass through definite types of property relations. Given the prevailing property relations (i.e., social system), our survival instinct brings about incremental improvements in the productive forces. The (historical) purpose of those improvements is to continue to reduce our dependence on nature. However, at some level of economic development, the prevailing property relations will become a fetter to further improvements in the productive forces. Then and only then, the prevailing social system would have performed its historical function. As the old system breaks down, a qualitatively new set of property rights will emerge. This new system will accelerate improvements in the forces of production (i.e., economic development). But, at some level of economic development, the system that was initially a progressive one will once again become an obstacle to further improvements in the forces of production. The cycle repeats itself until the final stage of communism is reached. According to Marx, in its journey through history, mankind must pass through definite types of property relations (i.e. socio-economic systems). A system cannot be born before the old one has performed its historical function.

Historical evidence, the economic performance of capitalist states, the economic (non) performance of socialist states, and the bankruptcy of socialism in the former Soviet Union and Eastern European support neither Marx's analysis of the process of social change nor his thesis that socialism is inevitable.

THE INEVITABILITY OF SOCIALISM

The thesis of the inevitability of socialism has its origin in the thought of Karl Marx. Unlike early socialists, Marx saw the institutions of socialism emerging spontaneously in the wake of capitalism. And he thought that their emergence was an inevitable outcome of the process of social change. According to Marx, socialism is to replace capitalism at the right time. And the right time is when there is no more room for the productive forces to develop within the capitalist relations of production.

It is probably safe to assert that few people today subscribe to Marx's thesis of the inevitability of socialism. Empirical experiences with all kinds of socialist institutions-- ranging from those of the former USSR to those in Cuba, the former Yugoslavia, Allende's Chile, and China-- have not been very helpful in upholding the faith in the inevitability of socialism. To salvage Marxism, socialists have to rewrite Marx's doctrine.

Hans Albert and Karl Popper, among others, provided a theoretical explanation of why empirical evidence refutes the thesis of the inevitability of socialism. Their refutation is based on two premises, which are only summarized here. The first premise is that the course of human history is strongly influenced by the growth of human knowledge. Expanding knowledge creates new technical opportunities which, in turn, affect human wants, change our attitudes and, in general, lead to consequences that cannot be anticipated. The second premise is that we cannot predict, by rational or scientific methods, the future growth of our scientific knowledge. A critical implication of these two premises is that the future course of human history cannot be predicted. Albert wrote:

> [It] follows that it is impossible to predict the course of history and that advances in science cannot remove this impossibility because science itself is an important cause of this unpredictability. As it were, the development of human culture is the continuation of biological evolution by other means. Instead of mutation we have innovation; instead of hereditary transmission we have a kind of evolution by tradition....Just as we cannot predict mutations in detail...we are not able to predict genuine innovations, even if we have sufficient theoretical and historical knowledge about the

problem-solving behavior of the individuals and about the social mechanism involved.[1]

SUGGESTED READING

Briton, C. The Shaping of the Modern Mind, New York: New American Library of World Literature, 1959.

Feuer, L. (ed.) Marx and Engels, Basic Writings on Political Philosophy, Garden City: Doubleday, 1959.

Manchester, W. A World Lit Only By Fire, Boston: Little, Brown and Co, 1993.

North, D. and Thomas, R. The Rise of the Western World, Cambridge: Cambridge University Press, 1973.

Weber, M. The Protestant Ethics and the Spirit of Capitalism, New York: Scribner, 1960.

[1] Albert, H. "Is Socialism Inevitable?" in Socialism: Institutional, Philosophical and Economic Issues (S. Pejovich, ed.), Dordrecht: Kluwer Academic Publishers, 1987, pp 56-7.

Chapter 3

INSTITUTIONS

INSTITUTIONS: DEFINITION AND PURPOSE

Exchange and production are major methods by which people seek to resolve problems that have their source in scarcity. The complexity of the environment, the computational limitations of the individual, and our inability to predict the behavior of others affect each individual's capacity to understand, process, and utilize information about the environment. Individuals' perceptions of the real world are colored by their values, experiences, traditions, observed successes and failures, and reason. Dedication to ideologies, sacrifice in defense of abstract causes, depth of religious beliefs, and many other observed behaviors of individuals and groups can be neither internalized in terms of neoclassical theory nor dismissed as ad hoc events. Those behaviors are evidence of the individual's subjective perceptions of reality.[1]

Given their subjective perceptions of reality, individuals develop institutions or "rules of the game" to reduce the uncertainties involved in human interactions.

In the pursuit of survival, small groups institutionalized into sets of customary rules their past experiences, taboos, and other perceptions they had formed about the world around them. Members of those groups lived together and interacted with each other. Interactions with members of other groups were rare and usually not

---

[1] The behavioral assumptions of neoclassical theory rests on the assumption that competitive forces assure an efficient outcome, and that the system can best be understood in terms of the analysis of predetermined equilibria. However, it is difficult to reconcile neoclassical theory with the performance of various economies. Why are inefficient alternatives surviving? Why does the same set of rules imposed in different countries produce different outcomes?

very friendly. It was then easy to detect deviations from the prevailing rules. Consequently, the enforcement costs of customary rules were low.

In time, the development of new trade routes and general improvements in knowledge created incentives for individuals in a given community to interact with members of other communities. In order to capture the potential gains from exchange, they had to enter into contracts with individuals whom they did not know, who followed different customs, and whose behavior they could not observe at a low cost. Yet, the growth of trade depended on the enforcement of intercommunity contracts. Driven by self-interest, kings, feudal lords and bishops rose to the challenge by replacing local customs with rules derived (mostly) from the christian ethics[1] As the extent of exchange and production rose, kings, lords and bishops claimed a major share of the resulting growth of wealth. Nowadays, constitutions, statutes, and common laws determine the rules of the game in modern states. By incurring the costs of enforcing contracts between total strangers (cotton produced in Australia might be used to make shirts in New York which are then sold to rangers in Montana), governments create opportunities for the growth of wealth and appropriate a share of those gains through taxation.

This means that economic activity involves human interactions at two levels. The first is the development and specification of institutions. The second level of economic activity involves human interactions within the prevailing institutions. The former is about the rules of the game, while the latter is about the game itself.

We define institutions as the legal, administrative and customary arrangements for repeated human interactions. Their major function is to enhance the predictability of human behavior.

---

[1] Religions and ideologies can be defined as sets of normative views that individuals develop as regards how the world should be organized. The difference between the two is that religion usually promises some sort of afterlife, whereas ideology is more interested in this time and space.

The prevailing institutional framework in a society consists of both formal and informal rules. Formal rules are constitutions, statutes, common laws and other governmental regulations which are externally enforced. They define the political system (the hierarchical structure, decision-making powers, the individual's rights), the economic system (property rights in scarce resources, contracts), and the protection system (judiciary, police, military).

Informal rules have their origins in the experiences, traditional values, ethos, religious beliefs, ethnicity and other factors that influence the subjective perceptions individuals form to interpret reality.[1] They are part of the heritage or culture which is transmitted from one generation to another via teaching and imitation. Some informal rules develop to make formal rules less costly to use (e.g., interpretations of various statutes). Others are derived from tradition, ideologies and religious beliefs and could be in conflict with formal rules (e.g., ongoing debate on abortion in the US). The world around us is full of examples of informal rules that affect human behavior differently from one area to another and from one culture to another. Examples are business practices in the United States where there is distaste for outright bribery, and in some central and south American countries where it may prove essential; the position of single mothers--difficult anywhere--being socially accepted in France but cast out by their families in Turkey; the work ethic in Germany is quite a different story from the attitude toward work in Montenegro.[2] Current debate on abortion in the Unites States can be seen as an attempt to replace the prevailing informal rule, which allows women to have abortions at the costs of medical assistance plus their social rejection by some friends, with a formal rule that would substantially increase the costs of unwanted pregnancies.

---

[1] Boyd, R. and Richerson, P.J., Culture and Evolutionary Process, Chicago: Chicago University press, 1985, p. 2.

[2] The costs an individual has to bear for violating informal rules might range from having to put up with unhappy neighbors to literally being expelled from the community.

Formal rules also can differ in impact from place to place. The development of representative bodies in sixteenth century Spain and England led to different rates of economic growth in those two countries.[1] Similar formal rules in the USA and many South American countries have produced different outcomes. Privatization laws in post-1989 Eastern Europe are having different results from one country to another. Japanese culture has survived the Americanization of the country. Serbs preserved their customs through five centuries of Turkish rule. Many "boat people" in the United States have managed to prosper under a set of formal rules they could not possibly have understood. And in Shasta County, California, the residents rely on a set of informal rules rather than legal norms to resolve disputes arising from damages done by stray livestock.[2] Douglass North wrote:

> The US Constitution was adopted with modifications by many Latin American countries in the nineteenth century, and many of the property rights laws of successful Western countries have been adopted by Third World countries. The results are, however, not similar to those in either the United States or other successful Western countries...the enforcement mechanism, the norms of behavior, and the subjective models of the actors are not [the same].[3]

Evidence shows that informal rules matter, that similar formal rules imposed on different societies produce different outcomes, and that informal rules have frequently outlived formal rules.

---

[1] See chapter 5.

[2] Ellickson, R, "Of Coase and Cattle: Dispute Resolution Among neighbors in Shasta County," Stanford Law Review, 1986, 38, pp. 624-87.

[3] North. D. Institutions, Institutional Changes and Economic performance,, Cambridge: Cambridge University press, 1990, p. 101.

CHANGES IN INSTITUTIONS

Friedrich Hayek generalized the history and development of institutions into the French or rationalistic tradition and the British or empirical tradition. The French tradition had two tenets: that there exists a "just" society in which people can live in peace and harmony, and that human reason is capable of discovering the institutions required to bring about such a society. The French tradition provided the philosophical rationale and political justification for governments to develop and impose outcome-oriented (exogenous) rules of the game. It also encouraged systematic investment in knowledge specific to social engineering.[1] Antitrust laws, labor laws, and regulatory agencies such as the Federal Trade Commission are a few examples of such developments in the United States.

Exogenous changes in institutions are usually conceptualized by scholars, advocated by various pressure groups, designed by lawyers, enacted by elected officials, and carried out by bureaucrats. The effect is to force the game to adjust to new rules. Exogenous changes are usually justified by reference to justice, fairness, morality, and/or the public interest. The problem with these terms is that none of them has a well-defined (agreed upon) empirical content. For example, if we assume that Bill Clinton and Ronald Reagan both acted in good faith during their respective years in the White House, the public interest is surely a very elusive concept. It is defined by individuals who, like all other individuals, have their own preferences, values, and private ends. And whatever the facade of words, a major effect (if not purpose) of exogenous changes in the rules is redistribution of wealth.

Using history as a guide, we can identify three general approaches to exogenous institutional changes: holistic, ideological or utopian, and creeping or incremental.

Holists tend to generalize historical events and personalities into prophesying the direction of social and economic development in

---

[1] The term social engineering could be defined as the process of developing and making exogenous changes in the rules of the game.

society. Hence, why not give the community a push in the right direction? Examples of holists are members of the German historical school, Hegel, Marx and Schumpeter. Holistic approach to social restructuring can be (and has been) easily radicalized. Lenin, Stalin, Mao and Castro are good examples. *Utopians* believe that we can use reason to discover the "just" society. Critical requirements that utopians have to deal with are: (i) Who is to identify the just outcome? (ii) What kinds of institutions would channel human behavior in the direction of that outcome? (iii) How to suppress competing institutions without eliminating democracy? Examples of utopians are pre-Marx socialists, the political elite in most third world countries, and supporters of the so-called Industrial Democracy in the West. *Incrementalists* seek to restructure society by way of marginal changes in the rules of the game. Examples include hiring quotas, minimum wage laws, etc.

The central premise of all advocates of exogenous institutional changes is that the price of social restructuring is worth paying. The problem is that they seek to satisfy their vision of a "good" community at the expense of its members. G. Warren Nutter used to define social and economic planning as a hazy vision of things that would be nice to have. And Hayek argued that the widely held ideas about bettering our lot via social and economic planning, more equal distribution of wealth, and the replacement of the competitive market process by a body of social engineers are all based on superstition.

The British tradition grew out of a strong dose of skepticism in either the rulers' foresight or their goodwill or both. Instead of searching for institutions that are outcome-oriented, the British tradition emphasizes the right of individuals to pursue their private ends. The rules of the game then emerge spontaneously via repeated voluntary interactions. Because of their voluntary acceptance, such rules are both self-sustaining as well as fair. The role of the state is to be limited to monitoring and enforcing those rules--a role not too different from that of the referee in a football game.

Hayek's arguments in support of the British tradition are well known. The rules of the game are the result of a process of selective evolution and maintain themselves by incremental adaption to changes in the environment. Individuals accept those rules not because they understand them but because they are advantageous to them. That is, human reason didn't create the rules but the rules made human reason possible. Reason appeared when the rules of the game began to include models of the environment that enabled individuals to explain and predict events. In a paper on the Hayek's vision of spontaneous institutional changes, Angelo Petroni wrote:

> The fact that the mechanism of evolution, when large numbers and long periods of time are involved, may be treated by the economist as if it were a Darwinian one, does not imply that individuals do not have a purposive objective-seeking behavior including imitation of others' successful behavior.[1]

The prevailing set of institutions in any society is a mix of spontaneous and exogenous rules. While it is not always easy to determine whether an institution is endogenous or exogenous, a helpful hint is that institutions that emerge spontaneously tend to be noncompulsory (e.g. the rule of limited liability, stock-exchanges, etc.). However, some endogenous rules are mandatory, like driving on the right-hand side of the road.

Both traditions confirmed that ideas have consequences. The French tradition created the market for social engineering and contributed, perhaps unintentionally, to the rise of socialism. The British tradition made a major contribution to the rise of classical liberal philosophy and methodological individualism.

STABLE AND CREDIBLE INSTITUTIONS

A major function of the rules of the game is to reduce the cost of human interactions through making human behavior predictable. To

---

[1] Petroni, A. "What is Right with Hayek's Ethical Theory?" paper.presented at the Mont Pelerin Society meeting in Cannes, September 25-29, 1994, p.26.

accomplish this objective, institutions must be credible (i.e. enforced) and stable.

The enforcement problem arises from increasing specialization and division of labor. By pushing out geographical frontiers, specialization and division enhance the extent of exchange. However, specialization and division of labor also increase transaction costs. It is then essential to develop and enforce institutional structures that enable individuals to take actions involving complex relationships with other individuals far removed from personal knowledge and extending over long periods of time.[1]

From an individual standpoint, rules yield a flow of benefits. The source of those benefits is the predictability of other people's behavior. Rules are also costly. The cost of a rule (formal or informal) is the satisfaction a person has to give up by not being able to engage in the activity which the rule constrains. My knowledge that other drivers will stop at a red light is my benefit from the rule. The fact that I must observe the same rule is the cost I bear.

As time goes by, individuals become better acquainted with the rules. They learn how to adjust to the system, identify exchange opportunities, and exploit the most beneficial ones. Thus, the flow of benefits from institutions depends on their stability and credibility (enforcement). For example, as long as university X has a well-defined set of rules, seniors are likely to capture more benefits from those rules than are sophomores. However, if the school changed its rules every year, the never-ending process of "learning" them would reduce their flow of benefits for all students.

The purchase of land, investments in various assets, and many other exchange opportunities have long-run consequences. Frequent changes in or expectations about changes in the rules of the game tend to increase the risk and uncertainty associated with those decisions, and raise their costs relative to contractual agreements that have a shorter time horizon. Jews in medieval Europe favored

---

[1] North, D. "Institutions, Economic Growth and Freedom," in Freedom, Democracy and Economic Welfare (M. Walker, ed.), Vancouver, B.C.: Fraser Institute, 1988, pp 5-7.

investments in jewelry and gold coins. South Americans prefer lower rates of return from (relatively stable) investments in the United States to the much higher (but often much riskier) rates of return that are often available in their homelands. An investor in post communist Russia seeks a shorter payoff period than that available in Germany. A stable and credible set of rules provides incentives to individuals to exploit the most beneficial exchange opportunities regardless of their time horizons.

Comparison with a football game may illustrate the point. In football, the rules of the game are set. Fans enjoy watching the game. Players know how to play it. And coaches know how to prepare their players. However, during an important game the blue team is on the one-yard line and fails to execute the fourth down. The coach goes to the referee and pleads: "My players worked so hard to get to the goal line, please give them another down?" Suppose the referee has power to choose to go along with the request, and the blue team wins the game. In the short run the team won. But frequent changes in the rules must cause problems for the game downstream. Football fans would not be able to enjoy the game, players would not know how to prepare for it, and football clubs would seek coaches who are better at getting rules changed than at coaching the players.

THE DIRECTION OF CHANGE

Let us now provide a very general sketch of what the process of spontaneous institutional change might look like. The agent of the process of change is the individual. In the pursuit of their private ends, individuals compete for scarce goods. The competition is carried out by means of institutions whose critical function is to reduce the costs of exchange and production.

The competitive process is, in effect, a *knowledge-creating process*. It continuously creates new opportunities for exchange and production. Examples of opportunities that the process creates are the opening of new markets, discovery of new sources of supplies, development of new technology, and changes in relative scarcities. An implication is that new knowledge affects relative prices. And changes in relative prices create new exchange opportunities. In order to capture potential gains, individuals and organizations may have to seek and negotiate new types of contracts. If the prevailing rules are poorly attuned to such contracts, negotiation and enforcement could turn out to be costly. The demand to reduce the costs of exploiting new opportunities, then, creates pressures from within the old system to change the rules of the game.

Those who stand to gain from changes in the rules have incentives to bear the costs of institutional restructuring. And those costs could be significant. Changes in formal rules may require a costly effort in terms of time and resources (including overcoming of free-rider problem). Changes in informal rules are less costly (losing some contracts, offending friends, etc) although the tenacity of informal rules could create a long-run problem. Changes in informal rules can be made by ignoring them, through their erosion, or through replacement by formal rules.

For example, changes in the opportunity costs (i.e. relative price) of being a homemaker in the United States led to a huge increase in women's participation in the labor force.[1] This change created opportunities for many individuals (not only women) to earn a differential return. In order to capture potential gains individuals had to try out new types of contractual arrangements. And those contracts that ended up earning differential returns were imitated by others. Eventually, the rules of the game adjusted to embrace successful contracts. All this led to changes in informal rules (e.g., social acceptance of the Pill, single motherhood, and live-in arrangements) and formal rules (e.g., abortion laws, and simplified divorce proceedings). Those changes in the norms of behavior are not a consequence of changes in our morals. The sequence is the other

---

[1] While a number of factors caused a change in the opportunity cost of staying at home, the growth of output had to be a critical one.

way around. Changes in relative prices, via voluntary adjustments in formal and informal rules, modify the prevailing ethical standards.[1]

There are basically three ways for the community to respond to a demand for a change in the rules of the game. *The allocative efficiency* refers to adjustments within the prevailing institutional framework (e.g., Gorbachev's perestroika). We observe this method of responding to demand for changes in the rules whenever the prevailing establishment has greater bargaining strength than those who expect to profit from institutional changes.

The adaptive efficiency method is to allow individuals and organizations to seek and negotiate new kinds of contracts and then institutionalize those that are repeatedly observed. Changes in the rules are both incremental and spontaneous. The law of *limited* liability is a good example of the adaptive efficiency. Technological developments in the nineteenth century made mass production of goods relatively cheap and profitable. To exploit new opportunities, entrepreneurs had to pull together large amounts of capital to finance start-up costs of production. However, the law of *unlimited* liability raised the costs of pulling together privately owned resources. It was costly for a person to be an absentee owner or to take on too many partners. Pursuing their self-interest, individuals responded to the problem the prevailing rule imposed by negotiating with creditors a variety of contracts which limited their liabilities. Some agreements passed the market test and were eventually institutionalized into the law of limited liability. The law limited the liability of individual investors to the market value of their investment in the enterprise. By reducing the cost of pulling together privately owned resources and allowing individuals to choose the amount of money at risk, the rule of limited liability enhanced the rise of the modern corporation. It also shifted the cost of evaluating business ventures to the creditors such as banks, brokerage firms and other financial institutions; that is, to those who specialize in evaluating investments.

---

[1] Some people see those changes in the norms of behavior as a decline in morals. Others see them as voluntary adjustments to changes in the economic conditions of life.

The piecemeal social engineering method of responding to demand for institutional restructuring requires the government purposefully to design and implement changes in the rules. The results of using piecemeal social engineering depend on the balance of bargaining power between the establishment[1] on the one hand and individuals and organizations demanding a change in the rules on the other. Changes in the rules are incremental but not spontaneous.[2]

WHY DO INSTITUTIONS DIFFER?

Our discussion does not suggest that more efficient institutions tend to replace less efficient ones. And for a good reason. We do not observe such a tendency in the real world. We observe the growth of institutional arrangements that enhance the growth of wealth. We also observe the growth of rules that restrict exchange and production. How do we explain the fact that more efficient institutions have failed to drive less efficient ones out of existence? Why do less efficient institutions manage to survive?

Major reasons for observed differences in institutional structures are twofold. First, politicians prefer specific to unintended outcomes. To get those results, the political elite must discover institutions that are specific to intended outcomes, and then implement them by fiat, and protect them from competition by alternative rules of the game. The political elite thus has incentives

---

[1] In case of Russia, the establishment is still a mix of old nomenklaturists and middle level bureaucrats. The transition problem in Eastern Europe is discussed in chapter 4.

[2] A good example is the development of telecommunications in the United States and Western Europe. U.S. rules were plastic enough (e.g., break-up of AT&T) to encourage individuals and groups to explore alternative ways of exploiting new technological opportunities. Consequently, the system moved in the direction of adaptive efficiency. In Europe, the establishment had much greater bargaining strength and the system moved in the direction of allocative efficiency with only minor changes in the rules. However, recent developments in Europe suggest that the results of the competitive process in the United States have been noticed.

to influence the demand for knowledge specific to the desired outcome by way of jobs, grants, and various subsidies. And scientists and educators have incentives to respond to this derived demand for knowledge by modeling institutional arrangements that promise to produce intended outcomes. Codetermination in Germany, regulatory agencies in the United States, and institutionalized protectionism in Japan are good examples.

Second, in a free society, people respond to opportunities for exchange by trying different types of contracts. The collective set of actual choices then approximates a random selection of contractual arrangements, from which "successes" and "failures" are chosen. With uncertainty and incomplete information, individuals interpret the results of different types of contracts differently. This means that all arrangements producing positive gains are eligible for imitation. Armen Alchian wrote:

> [I do] not regard uncertainty as an aberrational exogenous disturbance, as does the usual approach from the opposite extreme of accurate foresight. The existence of uncertainty and incomplete information is the foundation of...analysis; the importance of the concept of a class of "chance" decisions rests upon it; it permits of various conflicting objectives; it motivates and rationalizes a type of adaptive behavior; yet it does not destroy the basis of prediction, explanation, or diagnosis. It does not base its aggregate description on individual optimal action; yet it is capable of incorporating such activity where justified.[1]

The above discussion explains the persistence of rules having varying degrees of efficiency. But why do inefficient rules that restrict the growth of wealth continue to survive both in industrialized and developing countries? According to Paul David and Douglass North, "the path-dependence" is an (observable) answer.

---

[1] Alchian, A. "Uncertainty, Evolution, and Economic Theory," Journal of Political Economy, 58, 1950, p. 221.

Institutional changes have high transaction costs. The sources of those transaction costs are both subjective and objective. The former include the individual's perception of reality, notably shaped by the prevailing institutional framework. The latter are sunk investments in the prevailing set of formal and informal rules, the bargaining strength of the establishment, and imperfect markets. An implication is that the individual has incentives (except in the case of a major change in relative prices) to make marginal adjustments in the prevailing rules. Indeed we observe communities all over the world moving along inefficient paths even though aware of more efficient institutional structures elsewhere. There is no built-in mechanism for more efficient rules to replace inefficient efficient ones.[1] The entire transition process in Eastern Europe, including the rising strength of socialist parties in the region, is a good example of the thesis that history matters. We address that issue in chapter 4.

Institutions also have a tendency to outlive their usefulness. Many institutions have evolved into their present forms from serving a once important purpose. The convention of showing an open hand in greeting a stranger, at one time served to show that one was not bearing a weapon. By linking their present functions with originating circumstances, institutions give the hand of the past continuing leverage on the present. They become the "carriers of history." Paul David addressed the issue of why history matters in the evolution of institutions as follows:

> I perceive there to be three main analytical insights concerning the roots of path-dependence in economic phenomena which can take us a long way toward understanding why history matters so vitally where human organizations and institutions are concerned. The first has to do with the role of historical experience in the formation of structures of mutually consistent expectations that enable coordination to be achieved without centralized direction of the individual economic agents. The second is concerned with

[1] D. North, Institutions, Institutional Changes, chapter 11.

> ...the resemblance between the information channels and codes that organizations require in order to function with even a minimum level of economic efficiency. The third involves ...the necessity of achieving consistency and compatibility among the constituent elements of human organizations.[1]

Professor David's second point is especially interesting. It says that organizations develop their own "cultures," which have all the characteristics of capital assets specific to those organizations. For example, if I get a job with Texas Instruments I will have to master that firm's culture, which includes communication channels, information-processing procedures, and other internal codes. My knowledge of the Texas Instruments culture, which is of little value elsewhere, becomes part of the firm's capital stock. Both the firm and I have incentives to maintain this culture into the future.

SUGGESTED READINGS:

Alchian, A. "Uncertainty, Evolution and Economic Theory," Journal of Political Economy, 58, 1950.

North, D. Institutions, Institutional Changes and Economic Performance, Cambridge: University of Cambridge Press, 1990.

---

[1] David, P. "Why Are Institutions the 'Carriers of History'?" Paper presented at the Stanford Institute Symposium on "Irreversibilities," July 1992. p. 6.

CHAPTER 4

LAW AND INSTITUTIONS

THE RULE OF LAW

The rule of law can be taken to mean absence of arbitrary power and subjection of all citizens to the same laws. The absence of arbitrary power on the part of the government hinges on whether police powers are used to enforce the rights of individuals or whether they are used to enforce "people's" rights.[1] The absence of arbitrary power implies that no rule should be enacted with the intent of helping or harming particular individuals.

The subjection of every individual to the ordinary law before courts as in the British tradition (inherited by the United States) means that all citizens, including high level officers of the state are subject to the same laws administered by ordinary and independent courts. The French or continental tradition is somewhat different. Special administrative courts are often given the power of deciding the cases between private citizens and state officials when the latter are acting in their official capacity. This arrangement creates an opportunity for officials to identify their side of the issue with the public interest. Bruno Leoni wrote:

> We can create an "administrative law" before which all people grouped in a certain category defined in the law will be treated in the same way by administrative tribunals, and side by side with it we can recognize a "common law" under which people, grouped in other categories, will be no less equally

[1] The term "people" is a facade for the rulers, politicians and social engineers to hide their private ends.

> treated by the ordinary courts...Instead of "equality before the law" all that we shall have will then be equality before each of the two systems of law enacted in the same country.[1]

The legal origins of constitutional principles also differ between the British and continental systems. The British tradition generalizes the principles of the constitution from specific decisions (precedents) entered by common law courts. As old precedents are dropped and new ones are added to the legal system, judge-made rules change the constitution *incrementally*.[2] Judge Posner explained the production of precedents as follows:

> When a case is decided, the decision is thereafter a precedent, i.e. a reason for deciding a similar case the same way. While a single precedent is a fragile thing...an accumulation of precedents dealing with the same question may create a rule of law having the same force as an explicit statutory rule....the body of precedents in an area of law is a stock of capital goods that yields services over many years to potential disputants in the form of information about legal obligations....The capital stock of precedents is the joint product of the lawyers and judges engaged in the argument and decision, respectively, of cases, mainly appellate cases.... Capital goods depreciate....accident law that was developed to deal with collisions between horse-drawn wagons will be less valuable applied to automobile collisions....As old precedents obsolescence, eventually ceasing to be a part of the usable

[1] Leoni, B. Freedom and the Law, Princeton: Van Nostrand. 1961. p. 69.

[2] The United States has inherited this tradition, as evidenced by (i) the importance of judicial decisions in adjusting the principles of the constitution to changes in the political, social and economic conditions of life, and (ii) a costly method of changing the constitution via the U.S. Congress.

stock of precedents, new ones are added to the stock through litigation.[1]

In the continental tradition, precedents have only indirect bearing. The principles of the constitution are written by experts, debated by groups of citizens, and eventually adopted by constitutional assemblies or regular parliaments. The rights and liberty of individuals are then deduced from the general principles of the constitution. However, parliaments have the power to modify the prevailing constitution and even replace it with another. It follows that the extent of individual liberties as well as the certainty of the rule of law today does not say much about what the rules of the game are going to be tomorrow. An implication is that the continental tradition has a bias against decisions that postpone the benefits far into the future.

COMMON LAW AND STATUTES

Common law and the legislative process are two major methods for modifying and changing formal rules in countries that respect the rule of law. Empirical and theoretical research have suggested that common law courts tend to make decisions that enhance efficiency, while legislative enactments show no such tendencies. This section summarizes some major research findings.

Legislation

The legislative process is directly influenced by the people who expect to be affected by proposed legislation. Suppose 100 people in a community support a rule (e.g., to allow a factory to emit smoke)

---

[1] Posner, R. Economic Analysis of Law, Boston: Little, Brown and Company, 1992, pp. 539-40. Posner says that the rate of depreciation of precedents is relatively low--4-5 percent.

because they perceive it to be worth $100 to each of them individually. The cost of that rule is borne by all members of the community, say 2,000 people, including the 100 beneficiaries. The cost of the rule per person is $7.[1] The rule is clearly inefficient because its total costs ($14,000) exceed its total benefits ($10,000).. Yet, it could pass. Those who benefit from the rule are willing to invest up to $93 in convincing legislators that the bill should be passed. Other members of the community will have incentives to invest only up to $7 per person to prevent the rule from being enacted.

The example is hypothetical but plausible. It merely demonstrates that an inefficient rule might easily be enacted. The beneficiaries are a small group with high individual stakes in the rule. Their costs of forming an interest group are positive but low relative to potential benefits. The losers are a large group with low individual stakes in blocking the rule. Their costs of organizing a pressure group are high relative to potential benefits. Indeed, it is possible that some members of the community might choose to bear the cost of organizing others, or some "professional" advocates supported by grants from foundations might take up the case.

The point is that the legislative process does not provide strong incentives to block inefficient rules.

In fact, the prevailing incentives favor inefficient rules. Legislators have a valuable property right, namely the power to confer the gains and to impose the costs on individuals. The legislative process, then, creates a market in which legislators could sell (or block) a redistribution of wealth in exchange for support and campaign contributions. It is predictable that individuals, organized groups and business establishments will try to influence public policy

---

[1] With uncertainty and incomplete information, individuals can only perceive the costs and benefits of decisions that have future value consequences. Thus, the costs and benefits perceived by each group are likely to be different. But even if the perceived costs and benefits were equal, the rule would still be inefficient. First, a political redistribution of wealth increases incentives of those who own resources to seek less efficient outcomes. Second, the credibility of the prevailing rules of the game would be reduced.

by making campaign contributions to specific legislators, paying high lecture fees, and providing them with a variety of other nonpecuniary benefits. An implication is that the problem is not interest groups but the ability of the state to use political power to reward some and penalize others.

A good example is the so-called "milk bill" in California. A representative in need of campaign contributions and other perks will introduce or help introduce a bill which constituents then "urge" that representative withdraw or try to defeat. As George Stigler notes:

> The state is a potential resource or threat to every industry in the society. With its power to prohibit or compel, to take or give money, the state can and does selectively help or hurt a vast number of industries.[1]

Common Law

Two different but mutually reinforcing lines of research have been pursued to explain why the common law is efficient. The first line of research starts with common law judges. It takes for granted that judges, like all other people, prefer more satisfaction to less satisfaction. The issue is then whether the prevailing incentives structures under which they work have an efficiency bias. The answer is a weak yes for three reasons.

Common law judges are under competitive pressure to seek efficient precedents. Inefficient precedents would result in replacement of courts with private arbitrations and out-of-court agreements.

Unlike legislators who deal directly with individuals and groups, common law judges deal primarily with activities. That is especially true of judges in the appellate courts where most precedents are made. By making it difficult for common law judges

---

[1] Stigler, G. "The Theory of Government Regulation." Bell Journal of Economics, 2, 1971, p. 3.

to seek a monetary payoff, the rules of the judicial process reduce the influence of various pressure groups.

Major sources of utility for common law judges are nonmonetary goods such as power, prestige, and leisure. They make judges sensitive to being reversed by higher courts and eager to contribute to new precedents. Posner notes:

> An odd feature of [the production of precedents] is that the producers are not paid. Neither the judges nor the lawyers in Hadley vs. Baxendale received any royalties or other compensation for a precedent that has guided the decision of thousands of cases....The costs to judges of professional criticism are modest, but because the rules of judicial tenure and compensation attenuate the usual incentives that operate on people, judges are likely to be influenced by what in most walks of life is a weak force.[1]

The system, then, provides some incentives for common law judges to conform to the prevailing mode of thinking about social and economic issues, to have a conservative bias in judging disputes in their courts, and to attempt to create precedents when they believe that those precedents have a chance to last.

The second line of research arises from Adam Smith's dictum that the efficient allocation of resources is the unintended outcome of voluntary interactions by utility-seeking individuals. It extends this proposition to legal disputes by saying that common law rules are the unintended outcome of decisions to litigate by self-interested individuals.

A decision to settle a dispute or to litigate depends on the stakes. For the plaintiff the stakes are subjective evaluation of the probability of winning the case times the value of the judgment minus litigation costs plus settlement costs, that is:

$$P_pJ - L_p + S_p$$

---

[1] Posner. R. Economic Analysis of Law. p. 541.

For the defendant the stakes are subjective evaluation of the probability of losing the case times the value of the judgment plus litigation costs minus settlement costs:

$$P_dJ + L_d - S_d$$

In a world of uncertainty, the stakes are not likely to be the same for both parties. Their evaluations of probabilities, perceptions of the working of the judicial system, and attitudes toward risk are likely to differ. However, the condition for litigation is

$$J(P_p - P_d) > L_p + L_d - S_p - S_d$$

If $(P_p - P_d)$ is zero or negative, litigation would be more costly than settlement and the case will be settled out of court. On the other hand, the larger the difference between P_p and P_d, the more likely it is that the case will end up in court.

For example, suppose that J = \$100,000, P_p =.8, P_d =.5, and L and S are equal for both parties at \$10,000 and \$3,000 respectively. The left-hand side of our inequality is \$30,000 and the right-hand side is \$14,000. In terms of their respective self-interests, the plaintiff will not accept less than \$73,000 to settle the case, and the defendant will offer no more than \$57,000. The stakes are significant and the case is likely to be litigated. How are decisions to litigate, like this one, expected to generate efficient rules?

The total set of rules in a community at any given time consists of efficient and inefficient rules. Given individuals' evaluation of their stakes, some rules are always being challenged in courts. Since efficiency means that the costs imposed by inefficient rules are greater than the costs imposed by efficient rules,[1] a larger

---

[1] For example, suppose A and B can avoid an accident at costs of \$1,000 and \$3,000 respectively. If B is liable for damages the amount invested in accident avoidance will be less (damages will have to exceed \$3,000 rather than \$1,000) and more accidents will occur. Where the cost of avoidance is made greater, the amount invested in avoidance will be lower.

proportion of contested rules will be inefficient. If the litigated rules are decided on some basis unrelated to efficiency of outcome, the common law efficiency will tend to increase over time. In a pioneering study R. Priest wrote:

> Efficient rules survive in an evolutionary sense because they are less likely to be re-litigated and thus less likely to be changed, regardless of the method of decision. Inefficient rules perish because they are more likely to be reviewed and review implies the chance of change whatever the method of judicial decision....the tendency of the common law over time to favor efficient rules does not depend on the ability of judges to distinguish efficient from inefficient outcomes....The tendency toward efficiency is a function of the common law process according to which legal rules are generated from the investment in litigation by individual parties and the parties' investment is systematically determined by the allocative effects of prior legal rules.[1]

New social and technological developments continuously create new issues. In a world of uncertainty and imperfect knowledge, interacting individuals, including common law judges, have their own subjective perceptions of those issues. And those perceptions can be expected to differ from one person to another. Thus, the process of searching for better rules is likewise continuous.

An implication of our analysis is that the efficiency of the common law precedents is merely a tendency.

---

[1] Priest, R. "The Common Law Process and the Selection of Efficient Rules," Journal of Legal Studies, 6, 1977, p. 72. Other pioneering studies on why the common law is efficient are: Cooter, R. and, Kornhauser, L. "Can Litigation Improve the Law Without the Help of Judges," Journal of Legal Studies, 9, 1980; Goodman, J. "An Economic Theory of the Evolution of the Common Law," Journal of Legal Studies, 7, 1978; Rubin, P. "Why Is the Common Law Efficient," Journal of Legal Studies, 6, 1977.

THE RULE OF LAW IN CAPITALISM AND SOCIALISM

Socialism relies on the ability of the political-scientific elite to identify the public interest and to develop the rules that are expected to attain it. Capitalism maintains that individuals are the best judges of their own ends. Where capitalism opposes the coercion of citizens so that they can instead pursue their private ends, socialism seeks to coerce individuals so that the community can attain the intended outcome. To paraphrase Hayek, socialism makes individuals a bare tool in the achievement of the ends of the political-scientific elite. A consequence is that politicians and bureaucrats in a socialist state have significant discretionary powers. Such power creates a political market in which individuals have to invest their time and resources either seeking favorable laws or averting unfavorable ones.

Socialism sees the free-market, private-property rights economy as encouraging selfishness and greed. Thus, legal rules are needed to avert "anti social behaviors." Capitalism, on the other hand, contends that it is not a function of law to modify individual choices and preferences. Any individual should be free to "purchase" an anti social behavior at a market price, which is the cost imposed on the individual by friends and neighbors.

The concepts of "fairness," "justice" and "morality" have different connotations in capitalism and socialism. A capitalist society puts a premium on the rules that reward performance, cultivate risk-taking attitudes, promote the development of individual liberties, and place value on the keeping of promises. In a socialist society, the terms fairness, justice and morality are used to justify laws that change the distribution of income, provide social insurance coverage, mandate educational choices, and impose price controls. Says George Stigler:

> I deny the existence of a widely accepted, coherent moral code in which non-coercion is an irresistible corollary. The assertion of moral values, in the absence of such a code, is

> either a disguised expression of personal preferences or a refusal to continue the analysis of a problem.[1]

Capitalism is a *process* within which individuals voluntarily interact in the pursuit of their own private ends and, in doing so, create an order. The spontaneous order that the market achieves is a way of life deriving its energies and behavioral incentives from the right of ownership, contractual freedom and a government under law. An important positive aspect of this spontaneous order is that the value of resources in their alternative uses is identified by the only source of value: *the individual.* James Buchanan wrote:

> Economic performance can only be conceived in values; but how are values determined? By prices, and prices emerge only in markets. They have no meaning in a non-market context,... where the choice-influenced opportunity costs are ignored.[2]

It is, therefore, misleading to consider capitalism and socialism as alternative "mechanisms" for the allocation of resources. They represent two different ways of life each having specific and predictable effects on the development of laws and regulations. Walter Williams, professor of economics at George Mason University, summarized this point as follows:

> Fascism, communism and socialism are kindred forms of collectivism whose survival critically depends upon undermining of private property rights, rule of law, limited government and other institutions that [define the way of life in a capitalist society]. Collectivists everywhere disdain the rule of law, traditions and the market place in favor of the

---

[1] Stigler, J. "Wealth, and Possibly Liberty", Journal of Legal Studies, 9, 1980, p.216.

[2] Buchanan, J. "General Implications of Subjectivism in Economics," Paper presented at the Conference on Subjectivism in Economics, Dallas, Texas, December 1976.

> direct pursuit of intended outcomes....The Bush administration's Americans with Disabilities Act and the Clinton health plan are large down payments on socialism. The emphasis is focused on promised results and not process, as collectivists do everywhere.[1]

In evaluating the institutions of socialism critical questions are: Can socialism establish the desirability of outcome-oriented laws? Are those outcomes attainable? At what costs? With respect to capitalism, important questions are: What are the incentives for the spontaneous development of laws? What are the expected consequences of those rules? And at what costs?

THE RULE OF LAW AND THE TRANSITION PROCESS IN EASTERN EUROPE

It is clear that in 1989, East Europeans wanted socialist rule to end. By mid-1990, pro-collectivist parties (communists, socialists, fascists) were doing well in free elections. The purpose of this section is to show that the transition process based on exogenous institutional changes is a major reason for the rising strength of those parties.

For several decades East Europeans were forced to live under a system that tolerated neither the free market for ideas nor contacts with the rest of the world.[2] As socialist rule ended, East Europeans were in no position to identify quickly alternative institutional arrangements and/or evaluate their expected consequences. There is evidence, however, that ordinary people in Eastern Europe were in favor of capitalism as they perceived the system. After several decades (seven in the former USSR) of Marxist indoctrination, East Europeans did not and could not see capitalism as a way of life in

---

[1] Williams, W. "Liberals Care Only About Results," Conservative Chronicle, February 9, 1994, p. 24.

[2] Yugoslavia was the only exception.

which each and every individual bears the value consequences of his or her decisions. The prevailing perception of capitalism was to identify it with bountiful supplies of goods and equally large incomes to buy those goods. The benefits of capitalism were somehow to be captured with neither a change in work ethic nor a reduction in the prevailing welfare programs. The transition process quickly disillusioned people about the system as they perceived it.

At the same time many of us in the West interpreted the end of socialism in Eastern Europe to be a vote for capitalism as we understand the system. Thus, we encouraged new leaders in Eastern Europe to use the strong hand of the state to "build" capitalism in their respective countries. From the standpoint of ordinary people in Eastern Europe, the transition process then became a substitution of one set of institutions for another set, neither of which they chose for themselves.

History Matters

Socialist rule in Eastern Europe subverted the rule of law to the will of the ruling elite and seriously undermined people's confidence in enforcement mechanisms. During the immediate post-1989 period, the prevailing socialist institutions have been destabilized. Perceiving an institutional vacuum, East Europeans needed a stable set of rules for carrying out transactions among themselves and with the rest of the world. And they began to fall back on their *informal* norms of behavior. With its emphasis on ethnicity, the extended family, and shared values, the old ethos was a powerful fortress; behind its walls most people had been able to hide and learn to live with socialist institutions without ever accepting them. An unintended effect of socialist rule, then, was to preserve the region's informal rules.

The behavior fostered by this tradition is, however, limited to a group of people who share the same traditions and values.[1] In Eastern Europe, those groups of people are usually members of the same ethnic group. Interactions within any specific group are thus subject to rules of behavior that do not necessarily hold in exchanges across ethnic lines. The Serbs in Croatia, the Albanians in Serbia, the Turks in Bulgaria, and the Hungarians in Romania are examples of ethnic groups seeking cultural autonomy.

Evidence is plentiful that the old ethos has affected the behavior of ordinary people toward capitalism in the transition process. They see the gains from exchange as a redistribution of wealth rather than as rewards that individuals receive for creating new value. State authorities are more likely to shutdown operators who earn large profits by producing and/or selling goods for which supplies are low relative to demand than to encourage others to emulate such individuals in open markets. Members of collective farms in Russia are making life difficult for farmers who choose to go private. Small shop owners in the Ukraine are treated as second class citizens. There is also a common conviction in Eastern Europe that resources are found rather than created. Thus, the accumulation of private wealth in many East European communities is suspect.

It is true that capitalism had to face similar problems in many other countries with strong collectivist traditions. Chile, Japan, South Korea and Taiwan, among other countries, have given their people opportunities to experiment with alternative institutional arrangements. People responded by exploiting various opportunities and adopted those that passed the market test. Eventually, most of those countries ended up with a blend of capitalist institutions and old traditions. On the other hand, new leaders in Eastern Europe, with considerable support from the West, used the strong hand of the state to "give"

---

[1] The rise of "ghettos" in many large American cities reflects a tendency on the part of ethnic, racial and religious groups to stay around those whose behavior they can predict. Street riots, zoning issues, civil disturbances and various forms of real or, more likely, perceived discrimination are predictable consequences of interactions between mutual aliens. Civil rights laws enacted in the second half of the twentieth century have raised the cost of ghettos in American cities.

capitalism to their people. And they have, except in a few countries, failed. An implication is that the method of choosing institutions matters.

As socialist rule ended in Eastern Europe, former leaders had incentives to seek ways to preserve their power and privileges. Their human capital qualified them for seeking advantages in a bureaucratic environment; therefore, a free-market, private-property system was a threat to their private well-being. To preserve the value of their human capital, former communists, while paying lip service to free-market reforms, somehow had to create a state-centered system. They realized that encouraging the perception of an external threat to their respective ethnic groups would give them their best chance to create such a system. Most former communists, then, quickly transformed themselves into nationalists. It was an easy thing for them to do because nationalism and socialism have one important common trait: the collectivist mode of looking at the world.

In general, nationalism represents the conviction that the community's common good transcends the private ends of its members. This implies that individuals can attain their greatest potential only through their nationality. Nationalism is thus incompatible with individual liberty and competitive markets.[1] Indeed, most leaders in the multiethnic states of Eastern Europe in the early 1990s were nonreformed communists such as Milosevic in Serbia, Kucan in Slovenia, Meciar in Slovakia and Kravchuk in the Ukraine. The case of Czechoslovakia in the early 1990s is good evidence. In their quest to retain power, former communists in Slovakia adroitly exploited Slovak nationalism, eventually separating the country into two sovereign states. In contrast, the Czechs, with

[1] It is important not to confuse patriotism with nationalism. Patriotism means attachment to a community and its tradition. However, it is compatible with a voluntary association of diverse individuals who choose to live together. Unlike nationalism, patriotism is consistent with individual liberty, pursuit of private ends, and cultural diversity.

virtually no former communists in positions of power, are treating ethnic issues as a nuisance that could only interfere with getting the country on the road to economic recovery.

The Cost of the Transition Process

East Europeans had no opportunity to save and invest in "owned" assets during socialist rule. Instead, the state provided them with assets *specific* to a non-private property economy. Those assets consisted of (i) a variety of welfare benefits such as job security, allowances for children, medical benefits, and subsidized housing; and (ii) the shortage economy.

Retired people and older workers (forty-five plus) find the returns from those assets irreplaceable. Hence they have incentives to oppose the transition from socialism to capitalism. Older workers see capitalism as a threat to their current and future benefits from the system-specific assets. They fear, and for good reason, that the reminder of their working life is not long enough to allow them to replace those benefits with private saving and investments. Retired people have already seen a decline in the value of their pensions and other benefits. In addition, the shortage economy made them an important asset to their families in two ways. First, they had time to wait in line for consumer goods. Second, they specialized in knowing what goods would be available, and where and when they were going to be available. Thus, they raised the real incomes of their families. As scarcity prices replace price controls, retired people fear that they will become a liability to their families.

Predictably, older workers and retirees perceive the transition from socialism to capitalism as a real threat to the value of their assets accumulated during socialist rule. They didn't purchase those assets by choice but that is all they got. Thus, a major segment of the population in Eastern Europe is hostile to capitalism for reasons of self-interest, whatever their ideological preference might be. Evidence is consistent with this proposition. Young people, who have made no investment in the old system's specific assets, are strong supporters of a transition to capitalism, while older workers and retired people tend to support pro-collectivist parties.

Implications of The Transition Process

A major characteristic of most transition models is that they endorse institutional changes, such as privatization of state factories[1] and the methods for organizing production,[2] that have to be introduced by **fiat**. Some spontaneous institutional changes have occurred in Eastern Europe. For example, private-ownership firms have emerged in most countries even though private property rights are yet to enjoy credible legal guarantees. However, exogenous institutional changes have dominated the transition from socialism to capitalism. What are some specific and predictable effects of exogenous changes on preferences of the median voter in Eastern Europe?

1. *Exogenous changes require an activist government as a means of imposing and maintaining them.* In Eastern Europe, the role of the strong hand of the state in the transition process is usually justified by reference to either the "public interest" or the efficiency-enhancing consequences of capitalist institutions. Both justifications are misleading.

The public interest argument assumes that the social welfare function exists and that public decision makers (could) know it. Neither assumption is derivable from scientific knowledge. An attempt to justify exogenous changes by reference to the maximization

---

[1] Most state factories in Eastern Europe have no chance to survive in competitive markets. Yet, we already observe that ordinary people fail to attribute dismal performance of those firms to the decades of communist mismanagement. Instead, they tend to say: "The free-market, private-property economy is not working either."

[2] For detailed analysis of the effects of exogenous changes on the choice of business enterprises see Pejovich, S. "A Property Rights Analysis of Alternative Methods of Organizing Production." Communist Economies and Economic Transformation,, 6, No.2, 1994.

paradigm of neoclassical economics conveys a message that capitalism is a "mechanism" for the allocation of resources, which, by implication, may or may not outperform alternative institutional arrangements. It is a bad message because the critical difference between capitalism and alternative arrangements, including socialism, is not in their quantitative performance but in their respective impacts on the way of life in society.

2. *Another consequence of exogenous changes is a contraction in the social opportunity set.*[1] Two factors are responsible for this outcome. First, exogenous changes interfere with "the constraints that are voluntarily arrived at when individuals are free to impose restrictions upon themselves."[2] Second, in a world of uncertainty and incomplete knowledge, social engineers and public decision makers do not and cannot possess reliable information about the economy's dynamic responses to exogenous institutional changes.[3] A dissipation of resources is then a predictable consequence of exogenous changes. In many East European countries, the effects of exogenous changes on the social opportunity set have revealed themselves via inflation and unemployment.

3. *Finally, the people who impose exogenous changes and those who implement them are not the same people.* The latter have considerable

---

[1] The social opportunity set is not confined to standard goods and services. It also includes all socioeconomicand sociopolitical institutions. See Jensen, M. and Meckling, W. "Rights and Production Functions: An Application to Labor-Managed Firms and Codetermination." Journal of Business, 52, No 4, 1979, pp. 470-2.

[2] Alchian, A. and Woodward, S. "The Firm is Dead: Long Live the Firm." Journal of Economic Literature, 26, 1988, p. 65.

[3] Human interactions continuously create and disseminate new knowledge. The assimilation and interpretation of this knowledge by different individuals keeps changing opportunity sets and expectations about future. To assume that individuals' utility functions are a given is thus misleading. They are continuously modified by the action-choosing process.

discretionary power in interpreting the intent of policy makers. They also have their own incentives and private ends that are likely to differ from those of their superiors. A predictable outcome in Eastern Europe has been a difference between the promised and observed results of the transition process.

The transition process through exogenous changes, then, could neither deliver the goods nor endear capitalism to East Europeans. Given their perception of the system, we should not be surprised that they feel that capitalism has failed them. The rising strength of pro-collectivist parties is therefore not a surprising consequence of the transition.

Conclusions

The transition process "imposed" some institutions of capitalism in Eastern Europe with little regard for the region's philosophical heritage, the way East Europeans perceived capitalism before 1989, the importance that well-defined groups attach to assets specific to the old system, or the role of local leaders in exploiting nationalism. Because they identify the results of the transition process with capitalism, East Europeans are voting free-market parties out of power.

An alternative approach to institutional changes in Eastern Europe is to let people choose their way of life. Spontaneous institutional changes cannot and would not guarantee that East Europeans will choose capitalism. However, the market for institutions would give them a chance to identify alternative arrangements, try them out, adjust to their consequences, and select those they prefer.

Indeed, we already observe thousands of small private firms--mostly kiosks and miniature shops--which have spontaneously emerged throughout Eastern Europe in spite of the absence of credible legal guarantees of private property rights. Many of those shops will not last but some will grow. While their economic significance is still modest, such private enterprises are the breeding ground for entrepreneurs, a work ethic, a capitalist exchange culture, and positive attitudes toward capitalism in general. They educate ordinary people to appreciate a way of life that rewards performance, promotes individual liberties, and places high value on self-responsibility and self-determination.

SUGGESTED READING

Cukierman, A. and Meltzer, A. "A Positive Theory of Discretionary Policy, the Cost of democratic Government and the Benefits of a Constitution," Economic Inquiry, 24, 1986.

Leoni, B. Freedom and the Law, Princeton: Van Nostrand, 1961.

Posner, R. Economic Analysis of Law, Boston: Little, Brown and Co, 1992, chapters 19 and 20.

Chapter 5

PROPERTY RIGHTS

DEFINITIONS AND TYPES OF PROPERTY RIGHTS

A growing body of analytical and empirical research has demonstrated that different property rights create their own specific incentives and transaction costs. In turn, those incentives and transaction costs have specific and predictable effects on human behavior. Economic analysis based on the effects of various property rights then contributes to better understanding of a wide range of real world events, demonstrates the relationship between alternative institutional arrangements and economic outcome, and provides refutable implications for its propositions.

Property rights are relations among individuals that arise from the existence of scarce goods and pertain to their use.

Property rights specify the norms of behavior with respect to scarce goods that each and every person must observe in interactions with others, or bear the cost of nonobservance. The prevailing system of property rights in the community then defines the position of each individual with respect to access to scarce resources.

This definition of property rights makes two important points. The first is that it is wrong to separate human rights from property rights.[1] My right to vote and my right to speak on political issues are my property rights because they define my position vis-a-vis other people. The second point derives directly from our definition of property rights. Suppose I own a computer. The right of ownership does not define the relationship between myself and the computer. It

[1] That is why W. Meckling prefers to use the term rights.

defines the relationship between myself and all other people as regards the access to the computer.

Categories of property rights are many.[1] The best understood are private ownership, state ownership and communal ownership. The effects of those rights on economic behavior are discussed throughout the book.

Private Property Rights

Writing on the concept of private property rights, Irwin Fisher said:

> A property right is a liberty or permit to enjoy benefits of wealth--in its broadest sense--while assuming the costs which those benefits entail...It will be observed that property rights, unlike wealth or benefits, are not physical objects nor events, but are abstract social relations. A property right is not a thing.[2]

The right of ownership contains three elements: exclusivity of ownership, transferability of ownership, and constitutional guarantees of ownership. Those three elements of private property rights have specific and predictable effects on economic behavior.

Exclusivity of Ownership. The exclusivity of ownership means that the owner has the right to choose what to do with an asset (e.g., the

---

[1] Roman law specified several categories of property rights: ownership (the right to use one's property within the limits of law), trespassing (the right to cross another's land), usus fructus (the right to use a scarce good belonging to someone else or to rent it to others, but not to sell it or change its substance), usus (the right to use a scarce good belonging to someone else, but not to rent it or sell it or change its substance), and pawn (the right to keep a thing belonging to someone else, but not to use it).

[2] Fisher, I. Elementary Principles of Economics,, New York: Macmillan, 1923, p. 27.

right to speak on a social issue), how to use it (e.g., to oppose abortion), and who is to be given access to it (e.g., to authorize an anti abortion league to speak for the owner). The owner, or a person the owner appoints, decides what to do with the assets; the owner captures the benefits of the decision, and bears its cost. The right of ownership then creates a strong link between one's right to choose how to use assets and bearing the consequences of that choice. The right of ownership is not an unrestricted right. But it is limited only by restrictions explicitly stated in the law. Such constraints on the right of ownership may range from substantial ones, such as price controls, to minor restrictions, such as keeping the fence around one's house two feet inside the property line. Whether we find those restrictions justifiable or not, their effect is to reduce the owner's set of choices.

By internalizing the costs of a resource, the right of ownership creates strong incentives for owners to seek the highest-valued uses for their resources. The world is full of observations that support this proposition. People take better care of homes they own than of those they rent. They are more likely to add oil to cars they own than to those they rent. I have two computers. The computer at home is mine while the one in the office belongs to the university. They render the same flow of services to me, yet I do not value them equally. I have more rights in the home, the car, and the computer that are mine.

Transferability of Ownership. The transferability of ownership means that the owner has the right to transfer an asset to others at mutually agreed upon terms. That is, the owner can sell the asset or give it away. What are some implication of this component of the right of ownership?

Suppose Ms. Smith is a farmer. She makes about $1,000 per year after direct expenses. Ms. Jones believes she could earn $1,500 farming the same land. That is, she believes she could produce a larger output. A transfer of the farm from a less productive Ms. Smith (who is using the farm the best she knows how) to a more productive Ms. Jones would maximize the value of production. The transferability of ownership provides incentives for the farm to be transferred to Ms. Jones. Assuming an interest rate of 10 percent, Ms. Jones would be willing to pay up to $15,000 for the farm, while Ms. Smith would have incentives to sell the farm at any price above $10,000.[1]

The Constitutional Guarantee of Ownership. Protecting private property rights from both majority rule and/or the ruling elite the constitutional guarantee of ownership divorces economic wealth from political power. In a non-private property society, people's economic well-being increases as they move up the power structure. If and when those same people get kicked out of the power structure, they lose economic benefits. The former Soviet Union and pre-1989 Eastern Europe are recent examples. The right of ownership breaks this link between political power and economic wealth in capitalism. The individual who loses political power does not lose his economic wealth.

Political power is not the exclusive road to economic wealth in socialism (e.g., athletes and artists were doing well in the former USSR), and the separation of power from wealth is far from perfect in capitalism. But, in general, a major consequence of the absence of private property rights is a marriage of political power and wealth, and a major consequence of the right of ownership is their divorce.

To summarize the effects of the three major elements of the right of ownership: Exclusivity provides incentives for owners to put their assets into the highest-valued uses; transferability provides incentives for resources to move from less productive to more productive owners;[2] and the constitutional guarantee of ownership separates the accumulation of economic wealth from the accumulation of political power.

---

[1] If Ms. Smith's subjective evaluation of the value of her farm exceeds $15,000, she would bear the entire cost of her decision not to sell the farm.

[2] In a world of uncertainty and incomplete information it is more accurate to say to more optimistic owners.

State Ownership

The term state ownership is merely a facade hiding the true owner, which is the political elite. State ownership is often called public or social ownership.[1] We observe many examples of public ownership in the United States, such as Hoover Dam, The Tennessee Valley Authority, national parks and military bases. Members of the political elite have the right to choose how to use state-owned resources, the right allocate the flow of pecuniary and nonpecuniary income from those resources, and the right to control who has what access to those benefits. State ownership provides the ruling group with two important rights: the right to appropriate a share of output for its own consumption and the right to allocate the remainder.

The cost of the goods produced by state-owned resources is the value of output that is forgone. With a few exceptions, those goods are sold below their costs. When we visit Yellowstone National Park, the entrance fee does not cover the cost of services we receive; that is, private costs we incur are below social costs of running the Park. The total social cost is spread over all taxpayers, including those who never visit the park. On the other hand, when we visit Disneyland, the price we pay has to be sufficient to cover the costs of running the place; that is, private costs approach social costs. Otherwise, the owner(s) would shift the resources to other uses. A consequence of state ownership is thus the presence of externality-- those who consume the good do not bear the entire costs of their consumption.

Public decision makers do not capture the benefits of their decisions, either. No matter what the state agency charges for its product, neither its officers nor their superiors can appropriate the residual after cooperating inputs (i.e., employees) are paid their contractual prices.

We can say that state ownership provides public decision makers with weak incentives to pursue efficient outcomes. Therein lies the problem with state ownership. Inefficiencies in government

---

[1] I am using these terms interchangeably.

have less to do with the professionalism, work habits or integrity of public decision makers than with the penalty-reward system arising from state ownership.

Communal Ownership

Communal ownership means that a well-defined group of people jointly holds a nontransferable asset. Ordinarily, members of the group have the right to decide how to use the asset and the right to allocate proceeds, But *they have no right to sell those two rights to others.* The rights are acquired by joining the group and lost by leaving it. In tribal communities, communal ownership in land was quite frequent. It still exists in many societies today. In modern times, various types of producers' cooperatives and labor-managed firms parallel such property rights.

Communal ownership has two important consequences. First, consider a group of 100 people who have the right to graze their cows on a pasture held in common. Each member of the group has a herd of 20 cows worth $100 per head. Given the amount of grass available on the pasture, grazing an additional cow would result in less weight per cow. And the price per cow would fall to $99. Suppose a member of the group decides to add a cow to *his* herd. The value of his herd would increase by $79, while the total value of all the cows owned by the other 99 group members would decline from $198,000 to $196,020. A decision by a group member to increase his herd by one cow shifts some of the costs to others. Common ownership, then, creates incentives to overutilize assets. Moreover, any attempt to regulate the use of assets held in common would merely create a costly bureaucracy as well as incentives for members of the group to cheat and lie.

Second, an individual captures a share of the benefits from resources held in common only through membership in the group. In a world of uncertainty and incomplete information, no individual can be sure of expected length of continuing group membership. Hence communal ownership creates a bias against decisions that have long-run consequences. The effect of the time horizon on the use of resources held in common is discussed in chapter 13.

THE DEVELOPMENT OF PROPERTY RIGHTS

Let us begin with goods that are free for all. In general, a good is free for all when the costs of establishing, policing and enforcing a right in that good are high relative to the perceived benefits from that right.

The rationing criterion for a free for all good is first-come, first-served. If I choose not to cut a beautiful young tree in a free for all forest, someone else will. My cost of "purchasing" that tree is the value of my time plus the (prorated) value of the tools I need to use to cut the tree. I do not have to pay the market price of the live tree. Externality is present because private costs of acquiring a free for all good are lower than are social costs. The rate of consumption of free for all goods should thus be expected to exceed the rate that would otherwise prevail if some kind of property rights in those goods were established and enforced.

The rate of investment in a free for all good is also affected. The investor has to bear the entire cost of policing and enforcing future benefits, perhaps even be willing and able to use violence to exclude all competitors. The rate of investment in free-for-all assets should then be expected to fall short of what the rate of investment would otherwise be if some kind of property rights in those assets were established and enforced.

Empirical evidence supports both propositions. One might ask why fishing, golfing and swimming are better at private lakes, private clubs and private beaches than at public lakes, municipal golf courses and free-for-all beaches? One might also wonder what happened to the buffalo, the whale, publicly-owned forests, and many rivers? If one is to blame human greed for the destruction of those resources, then why have the same presumably greedy humans preserved cattle, fertility of private farms, young trees in privately owned forests, clean water in private lakes, and many other scarce resources.

An implication is that individuals have incentives to exclude others from the free access (i.e., specify property rights) to a free-for-all good whenever *their* perceived benefits exceed *their* cost of policing and enforcing the "claim." And to exclude others from uncontrolled access to a good means to define property rights in that good. New property rights in a resource are then created and existing ones modified in response to changes in either the perceived benefits from those changes or the cost of defining, policing and enforcing new property rights in that resource. An unintended effect of this spontaneous change in property rights is to internalize some externalities and reduce the difference between private and social costs of using that good.

For example, in the early days of the Roman Empire a form of communal ownership called ager gentilicius developed. Agri gentilicii were pastures owned by the Gens (a group of people having the common ancestor), which all members exploited in accordance with their needs. As our analysis suggests, pastures owned by the Gens were overutilized. As agriculture developed in Rome, the value of crop growing rose relative to that of ranching and created incentives for parceling out the land into smaller units. In time, communal ownership in land broke down into consortiums, a form of nontransferable family ownership in land. Smaller family units captured more rights in their land, some social costs were internalized, and the difference between private and social costs was reduced.

This analysis of the development of property rights parallels discussion in chapter 4 on the development of common law and statutes. It suggests a tendency for more efficient property rights to develop spontaneously in response to the interaction between changes in the economic conditions of life and individuals' search for more utility. The role of the authority is a passive one and limited to enforcing new rules of the game.

However, history offers many examples of those in power assuming an active role in changing the prevailing property rights. The effect of exogenous changes in property rights is to force the game to adjust to new rules. While some exogenous changes in property rights might be prudent and justifiable, the problem is the same as with statutes: the power hierarchy compels people to accept new rules whether they like them or not. Central planning in the former Soviet Union, labor-managed economy in the former Yugoslavia, economic growth policies in many third world countries, and numerous environmental regulations in the United States illustrate this.

Theoretical and empirical research has identified a number of factors that create incentives for a change in the prevailing property rights. Some of those factors are technical progress, opening up of new markets, and changes in relative prices. In a paper on the development of property rights among American Indians in Quebec, Harold Demsetz wrote:

> Before the fur trade became established, hunting was carries out primarily for purpose of food and the relatively few furs that were required for the hunter's family. Externality was clearly present...But these external effects were of such small significance that it did not pay for anyone to take them into account. There did not exist anything resembling private ownership in land....The advent of fur trade had two immediate consequences. First, the value of furs to the Indians was increased considerably. Second, as a result, the scale of hunting activity rose sharply. Both consequences must have increased considerably the importance of the externalities associated with free hunting. The property right system began to change, and it changed specifically in the direction required to take account of the economic effects made important by the fur trade.[1]

[1] Demsetz, H. "Toward a Theory of Property Rights," American Economic review, 57, May 1967, pp. 351-352.

AN APPLICATION: PROPERTY RIGHTS AND ECONOMIC DEVELOPMENT IN ENGLAND AND SPAIN

In medieval Europe, the tradition was for a king to be self-sufficient. He was expected to live (and meet obligations to his subjects) on the income from his land and the traditional feudal taxes. However, changes in military technology, especially the use of gun powder, raised the cost of waging wars. A consequence was that the king needed additional sources of revenue.[1]

To get more revenues, the king had to turn to his subjects and offer protection of property rights in exchange for money. More secure property rights provided incentives to produce more goods, which the king could then tax. Clearly, a conflict of interest had to arise between crown and constituents with respect to distribution of the increment in output. The conflict led to the development of representative assemblies, their initial purpose being to represent the constituents in negotiations with the crown.

In those negotiations, both sides had incentives to seek the kind of contracts that would enhance their bargaining power. The crown preferred to resolve the conflict of interest with constituents within the prevailing institutional arrangements, which favored medieval guilds and the king's chartered monopolies. The assembly sought to reduce the king's discretionary powers through new institutions, that would give constituents legal protection.

At the beginning of the sixteenth century, institutional arrangements in England and Spain were similar and so were their respective levels of economic development. The wool trade was a major source of royal revenues in both countries. However, relative strength and opportunity costs of the crown and the assembly were not the same. And economic development proceeded along different paths in England and in Spain.

---

[1] North, D. "Institutions, Economic Growth and Freedom: A Historical Introduction," in Freedom, Democracy and Economic Welfare, (Walker, M. ed.), Vancouver, B.C.: Fraser Institute, 1988, pp.14-19. This summary of North's research is mine.

In England, the prevailing statutes covered only existing industries so that new industries were not bound by old rules. Moreover, law enforcement in the countryside was in the hands of judges who were not paid by the crown. Predictably, new industries moved into the countryside where guilds were much weaker, and price and wage controls were not effectively enforced. The result was the spontaneous development of joint-stock companies and growing resentment against the crown-sponsored monopolies. Eventually, political power shifted from the crown to Parliament. In exchange for the right to set taxes, Parliament guaranteed the king a stable flow of income. Toward the end of the seventeenth century, common law replaced old statutes as the law of the land. By helping to replace statutes with common law, competition among various courts with overlapping jurisdiction contributed to more secure property rights and local political controls. All of that helped to enhance economic growth in England.

In Spain, major sources of the king's revenue were the sheepherders' guild (Mesta), revenues from the empire, and sales tax. In return for the right of sheep owners to move their flocks around the country from one suitable pasture to another, Mesta guaranteed the king a stable flow of income. Consequences of this arrangement were insecure property rights in land and enhanced soil erosion both of which arrested the development of agriculture. As the balance of power shifted in favor of the crown, the conflict of interest between the crown and its constituents was resolved within the traditional institutional arrangements, and the country's economy declined.

SUGGESTED READING

Alchian, A. Economic Forces at Work, Indianapolis: Liberty Press, 1977, Part II.

Buchanan, J. The Limits of Liberty, Chicago: Chicago University Press, 1962.

Demsetz, H. "Toward a Theory of Property Rights," American Economic Review, 57, 1967.

North, D. "Institutions, Economic Growth and Freedom," in Freedom, Democracy and Economic Welfare (Walker, M. ed.), Vancouver, B.C.: The Fraser Institute, 1988.

Posner, R. Economic Analysis of Law, Boston: Little, Brown and Co, 1992, chapters 3 and 4.

PART TWO

PROPERTY RIGHTS, EXCHANGE, AND PRODUCTION

Chapter 6

THE COASE THEOREM AND TRANSACTION COSTS

THE COASE THEOREM

Using the case of Sturges vs. Bridgman,[1] Ronald Coase made two points: (i) clearly defined private property rights are an essential requirement for resolving the conflict of interests among individuals via market exchange, and (ii) an efficient allocation of resources is independent of the initial assignment of property rights as long as transaction costs are insignificant. He wrote:

> [Individuals,] who are normally only interested in maximizing their own incomes, are not concerned with social cost and will only undertake an activity if the value of the product of the factors employed is greater that their private cost...But if private cost is equal to social cost, it follows that [individuals] will only engage in an activity if the value of the product of the factors employed is greater than the value which they would yield in their best alternative use. That is to say, with zero transaction costs, the value of production would be maximized.[2]

---

[1] Coase, R. "The Federal Communications Commission," Journal of Law and Economics, 2, 1959, p. 25.

[2] Coase, R. "Notes on the Problem of Social Cost," in The Firm, the Market, and the Law (Coase, R. ed.), Chicago: University of Chicago Press, 1988, p. 158.

Suppose that Hamilton and Jefferson are neighbors.[1] Their homes are next to each other and they have been getting along quite well. Hamilton and Jefferson value their homes at $1,200 and $1,000 respectively. These are subjective values that may but may not equal market prices of the two homes.

One day, Jefferson gets an offer from the Scream & Scare, Inc. to test sirens in his kitchen in exchange for $500. Being indifferent to noise, Jefferson gladly accepts the offer.[2] Testing sirens imposes a subjective cost on Hamilton, say $200. Thus, the values Jefferson and Hamilton place on their homes in the two situations are:

Table 6-1. The Coase Theorem

	Hamilton	Jefferson	Total Value
No sirens	$1,200	$1,000	$2,200
Sirens	$1.000	$1,500	$2,500

Testing sirens in Jefferson's home creates a new issue that did not exist before. Externality is clearly present because the cost borne by Hamilton does not enter into Jefferson's cost-benefit calculations. Hamilton believes that he has the right not to suffer damages and wants Jefferson to stop testing sirens. Jefferson believes that testing sirens is a lawful activity and refuses to stop. Hamilton then takes Jefferson to court.

In order to internalize the emergent interdependence, the relevant property right must be defined. Before that is done, there is no way for Jefferson and Hamilton to negotiate a solution to their

---

[1] I owe this method of explanation of the Coase Theorem to R. Adelstein.

[2] We could also assume that Jefferson prefers $500 to whatever noise he has to put up with. Assuming that he is indifferent to noise does not change the results of our analysis, but eliminates the necessity of making an adjustment in Jefferson's net gains from accepting the offer.

dispute. What the court must decide is whether Hamilton has the right to impose additional costs on Jefferson by compelling him to stop testing sirens in his kitchen, or whether Jefferson has the right to impose additional costs on Hamilton by testing sirens in his kitchen. But Coase tells them: "It doesn't matter who wins; the result will be the same either way." Why?

Suppose Hamilton wins. Initially there will be no sirens. But the relevant property right is now defined. Jefferson knows that he is willing to offer up to $500 to purchase from Hamilton the right to continue testing sirens. While he might not know the value Hamilton places on that right, Jefferson has incentives to keep raising his offer until a deal is made. That would happen at some price between $200 and $500. Suppose Jefferson buys the right for $300. Then:

(i) Sirens are tested.
(ii) Hamilton is worth $1,000 + 300 = $1,300;
Jefferson is worth $1,500 - 300 = $1,200.
(iii) The value of production is maximized at $2,500.
(iv) Jefferson gets $200 and Hamilton $100 from the increment in total value of $300 ($2,500 - $2,200).

Suppose Jefferson wins. Initially there are sirens. Driven by his self-interest, Hamilton has incentives to offer up to $200 to buy the right from Jefferson. However, Jefferson will accept no less than $500. Thus, no deal can be made. Then:

(i) Sirens are tested.
(ii) Hamilton is worth $1,000;
Jefferson is worth $1.500.
(iii) The value of production is maximized at $2,500.
(iv) Jefferson gets $500 and Hamilton ($200) from the increment in total value of $300.

Coase is right. The sirens are tested regardless of the initial allocation of the relevant property right, and the total value is maximized ($2,500 vs. $2,200) either way. Hence, the Coase Theorem:

Where bargaining is relatively costless, an efficient allocation of the relevant property right (i.e., the one that maximizes the value of production) will be achieved regardless of the initial allocation of that right. But the distribution of this maximized value will differ from one initial allocation to another.

Suppose that the buyer of the right to test sirens has to pay a sales tax of $700. Then, the Coase Theorem would fail if the court has not granted the right to Jefferson initially.

If Hamilton wins, Hamilton is worth $1,200, Jefferson is worth $1,000, the value of production is *not* maximized at $2,200, and sirens are not tested because Jefferson cannot pay the minimum price of $200 plus the $700 tax.

However, if Jefferson wins, Hamilton is worth $1,000, Jefferson is worth $1,500, and the total value of production is maximized.

Hence, Posner's corollary: When transaction costs are relatively high, efficiency will result only if the court grants the right to the highest-valued owner.

TRANSACTION COSTS

The Coase Theorem says that the allocation of resources in the world of neoclassical economics[1] is independent of the legal assignment of property rights, which is an important but also a very limited proposition. However, the world of zero transaction costs *is not* a Coasian world. Coase's purpose has been to persuade his colleagues

---

[1] Standard economic theory assumes an instantaneous exchange that is costless to negotiate and enforce; ignores the costs of protecting and maintaining the institutional structure; and considers the set of maximum outputs (i.e., the production frontier) to be a function of the supply of inputs, their substitutability, and technology.

to leave the world of neoclassical economics and devote their energies to better understanding of the one we live in. He wrote:

> The reason why economists went wrong was that their theoretical system did not take into account a factor which is essential if one wishes to analyze the effect of a change in the law on the allocation of resources. This missing factor is the existence of transaction costs.[1]

Given their assumptions of private ownership in resources and zero transaction costs, neoclassical economists have developed a powerful apparatus for discussing *some* economic issues. However, analytical tools of neoclassical economics such as upward sloping supply and downward sloping investment schedules have frequently been used for economic analysis of social and economic issues in total disregard of transaction costs and incentives specific to alternative institutional arrangements. The problem is that the incentive effects of private property rights embodied in those analytical tools are not operative under alternative institutional arrangements and positive transaction costs, and neither supply schedules can be assumed to be upward nor investment schedules to be downward sloping. Thus, a mechanical extension of neoclassical analytical concepts and tools to non-private property and/or positive transaction costs environments is bound to produce misleading results. For example, SEC, FTC and many other regulatory organizations are unintended but predictable effects of neoclassical economics. Those agencies were formed to assure the economy of price-takers' competitive outcomes. Harold Demsetz wrote:

> The special notion of competition relied upon by the model [of perfect competition] makes that model a poor vehicle for understanding a wide variety of competitive tactics and institutions that are adopted precisely to accommodate ... uncertainty, and the cost of transacting. Particular marketing practices such as tie-in sales, reciprocity, and manufacturer

---

[1] Coase, R. The Firm, the Market, and the Law, p. 175.

> control of prices at which retailers resell their goods are difficult to explain with a model that assumes away their cause. Vertical integration and the very existence of firms find little rationale in the perfect decentralization model because their source lies in the uncertainties of real economic systems and in the cost of rising markets to accommodate to these uncertainties.[1]

Transaction costs are the costs of all resources required to transfer property rights from one economic agent to another. They include the costs of making an exchange (e.g., discovering exchange opportunities, negotiating exchange, monitoring, and enforcement), and the costs of maintaining and protecting the institutional structure (e.g., judiciary, police, armed forces).

Information about Exchange Opportunities is not a Free Good. In a world of uncertainty and incomplete knowledge, it takes real resources (including time) to produce information. College graduates know that it takes time and money to gather information about employment opportunities, but the search costs might prevent them from discovering the best alternative. Shoppers know that by driving around they can find the best bargains, but it might not be an efficient thing to do given the cost of gasoline and the alternative uses for their time. However, if the price at which a person can obtain additional information is reduced, additional exchange opportunities would be exploited and the extent of exchange increased. An important issue is then what set of institutional arrangements encourages activities that reduce transaction costs? Or, what are the effects of various rules of the game on transaction costs?

In a private-property, free-market economy, resources are devoted to producing and selling information. Real estate agents,

---

[1] Demsetz, H. Economic, Legal and Political Dimensions of Capitalism. Amsterdam: North Holland, 1982, p. 11.

employment agencies, advertising, marriage and dating bureaus, and scalpers are all engaged in the production of transaction services. Stores maintain inventories because it is a method for reducing the cost of information about fluctuations in the demand for their goods. The so-called "sticky" prices are a strategy on the part of the seller to reduce the cost of information to the buyer about the terms of exchange. It explains nothing to say that sticky prices, that is prices which do not respond to temporary fluctuations in demand, are a consequence of monopoly power,

The Costs of Negotiating Exchange Can be Quite Substantial. The parties may not know each other. They may not have all relevant information about goods and services. Goods and services have multiple attributes that affect their value. And it is costly to measure each and every attribute of the goods exchanged. A consequence of measuring all those attributes would be a reduction in the extent of exchange. The extent of exchange would also be reduced if the allocation of risk and other future consequences of each and every exchange had to be negotiated separately.

Market competition and the law of contract jointly reduce transaction costs in several ways. First, standardized contracts reduce transaction costs by enabling the parties to avoid the cost of negotiating the terms of contract for each and every exchange they make. When I go to a department store to open a credit account, I am invited to sign a contract that offers pre-determined (standardized) set of terms. How are those terms arrived at? Do they reflect a monopoly (take-it-or-leave-it) power of the store over me? Clearly, another store could compete for my business by offering better terms. Competition forces all stores to seek and offer contractual terms that satisfy preferences of the median consumer in their markets. Standardized contracts then emerge spontaneously as a method for reducing the costs of negotiating exchange.

Second, warranties, guarantees, return privileges and as-is purchases are a few examples of how market competition assigns in advance the risk of purchasing goods whose attributes cannot be immediately known. By holding people to their promises, the law of contract reduces the cost of negotiating exchange of those goods and services.

Third, with a few exceptions, the law of contract allows each party to choose between performing in accordance with the contract or compensating the other party for damages. It is an efficiency-enhancing provision. For example, A agrees to produce for B a number of ABC computers. Then a better line of computers (produced by C) becomes available and the market for ABC computers declines. Depending on costs, B can choose to cancel the contract and compensate A only for computers already produced and other sustained costs. This is an efficiency-enhancing provision in the law of contract. B has to pay A for resources actually committed to production under their contract. The completion of "unneeded" computers would have used additional resources, which is a waste.

Fourth, the law of contract reduces transaction costs by preventing opportunistic behavior. In Alaska Packers' Association vs. Domenico, the defendant hired a group of seamen to fish salmon off the coast of Alaska. The wages to be paid to the seamen were agreed to before the voyage. However, when the ship arrived in Alaskan waters, the seamen refused to work unless they were paid higher wages. Having no access to the labor market, the defendant agreed. But, upon return to San Francisco, he refused to pay his workers higher wages. The seamen sued and lost. The court held that the defendant's promise to pay the wages over and above the original contract was not supported by fresh consideration (reciprocal promise). This decision was efficiency-enhancing because it reduced incentives for opportunistic behaviors by contractual partners.

Richard Posner's comment on the court's decision in Alaska Packers' Association vs. Domenico was:

> As once it is well known that such modifications [in the contract] are unenforceable workers in the position of the

seamen in the Domenico case will know that it will do them no good to take advantage of their employers' vulnerability.[1]

Exchange is Costly to Enforce. Exchange can be simultaneous (e.g., buying fresh produce in a farmers' market) or over a period of time (e.g., I pay for my plane ticket before the airline fulfills its side of the bargain). In either case, but more clearly in the latter, problems with enforcing contractual agreements and of misunderstandings concerning the attributes of goods, the bundle of rights being transferred, and delivery dates are to be expected. An enforcement mechanism reduces the cost of exchange, eliminates the time horizon problem, increases the extent of trade, and provides incentives for resources to move to their highest-valued uses.

The market provides an enforcement mechanism. Those who repeatedly fail to perform their side of the bargain lose business to their competitors. A reputable dealer gets a higher price for the same good or service than a fly-by-night operator. Thus, a good reputation is an asset that has monetary value. A newcomer in town must be willing to trade at a lower price while investing in developing a reputation.

However, this selection process, important as it is, takes time and is costly. It is costly to many who act in good faith, to those who misunderstand the terms of exchange, and to the community as a whole because additional real resources have to be used to run credit bureaus, security deposits, and other means of self-protection. By enforcing exchange agreements, the law of contract enhances the market selection process and reduces transaction costs of exchange.

---

[1] Posner, R. Economic Analysis of law, p.87.

Empirical Estimates of Transaction Costs

Douglass North and John Wallis made the first comprehensive effort to measure transaction costs.[1] Predictably, the study questions more than it answers. Yet, North and Wallis gave us a conceptual framework to build on.

The study has three parts. The first section develops a theoretical definition of transaction costs and the transaction sector. The second section provides empirical estimates of transaction costs in the United States economy for the period from 1870 to1970. In the last section of the study, North and Wallis discuss potential implications of their empirical estimates of transaction costs.

The gains from trade are a consequence of specialization and the division of labor. They are realized through exchange which is not costless. An important implication is that transaction costs are a limiting factor on economic growth. It follows that incentives for efficiency improvements in the transaction sector are as important as those in the production sector.

According to their estimates, transaction costs have risen substantially during the period under investigation. Table 6-2 summarizes the results.

There are three major reasons for the expansion of resources used in the transaction sector of a growing economy. First, the expansion of markets and growing urbanization of the economy replaces repeated dealing with contractual partners we know with an ever-lengthening chain of exchanges carried out between individuals who have no knowledge of each other. Impersonal exchange requires more search and information-gathering activity as well as more elaborate enforcement mechanisms. Second, capital-intensive

---

[1] Wallis, J. and North, D. "Measuring the Transaction Sector in the United States Economy, 1870-1970," in Long-Term Factors in American Economic Growth (Engerman, S. and Gallman, R. eds.), Chicago: University of Chicago Press, 1986, pp. 95-161.

Table 6-2. The Transaction Sector as a Percentage of GNP

Year	Private Sector	Public Sector	Total
1870	22.49	3.60	26.09
1880	25.27	3.60	28.87
1890	29.12	3.60	32.72
1900	30.43	3.67	34.10
1910	31.51	3.66	35.17
1920	35.10	4.87	39.98
1930	38.19	8.17	46.35
1940	37.09	6.60	43.69
1950	40.30	10.95	51.25
1960	41.30	14.04	55.35
1970	40.80	13.90	54.71

Source: Wallis, J. and North, D. "Measuring the Transaction Sector in the United States Economy, 1870-1970," p. 121.

production techniques increase incentives for business enterprises to grow in size. An implication is that more resources have to be devoted to transaction services within the firm.

Finally, the gains from trade tend to create conflicting interpretations about the prevailing institutional arrangements as well as about the justice and fairness of the distribution of income in general and the increments of income in particular. Whether those conflicts emerge from differences in customs, ethnicity, religion and race or from occupational specialization and loss of personalized relationships between individuals in the community, more resources have to be devoted to defining and enforcing the rules of the game. North wrote:

> The gains from trade can only be realized by the establishment of contracts between principals or principals and agents which form the institutional framework of a political/economic system. Therefore, without some form of political order, organized trade cannot develop...With simple political and economic organization, custom may be sufficient to specify the structure with a consensus ideology. As the gains from trade that arise from specialization and the division of labor result in more and more complex forms of political and economic organization, the resource costs of capturing those gains from trade will increase. They will increase not only because the costs of measurement and enforcement of an ever-lengthening chain that result from greater and greater specialization will grow, but also because ideological alienation will characterize the relations between participants in the exchange process and will require greater and greater amounts of resources devoted to specification and enforcement of contracts.[1]

SUGGESTED READING

Alchian, A. "Some Implications of Property Rights Transaction Costs," in Economics and Social Institutions (K. Brunner, ed.), Boston: M. Nijhoff, 1977.

Coase, R. "The Problem of Social Cost," Journal of Law and Economics, 3, 1960.

---

[1] North, D. "Transaction Costs, Institutions, and Economic History," in (Furubotn, E. and Richter, R. eds.) The New Institutional Economics, Tubingen: J.C.B. Mohr, 1991, p.207.

Chapter 7

PRIVATE PROPERTY RIGHTS, EXCHANGE, AND PRODUCTION

Driven by the desire for more utility, individuals compete for scarce resources. Competition occurs at two levels. In chapters 3-5, we discussed "competition among rules." That is, the competitive process that is carried out by means of the development and choice of rules individuals adopt as the instruments with which they compete. In this and following chapters, we discuss "competition within prevailing rules." That is, the competitive process that determines the allocation and use of resources or, what is the same thing, the extent of exchange and production.

The competitive process within the prevailing rules is a knowledge-creating process. It continuously creates and spreads knowledge about opportunities for human interaction. This chapter discusses the implications of the right of ownership on the extent of exchange and production.

EXCHANGE

Exchange is a means by which individuals seek more satisfaction for themselves. The method of payment by one of the parties could be money or other goods; in exchange for using my lawn mower, a neighbor might drive my kids to school. People enter into exchange because they *expect* that their *benefits* from acquiring a good will exceed their *costs*. To understand the purpose of exchange it is important to understand the three terms emphasized here.

The benefit from exchange is the increment in satisfaction a person derives from acquiring the right to use a little more of any good. The value of any good to a person depends on the expected flow of benefits and the bundle of rights being transferred. Given the expected flow of benefits from a good, changes in the bundle of rights affect the price we are willing to pay for that good. The value of a car to me is less if I have no right to resell it; I pay more to join a country club if my teenage kids are allowed to play golf there; and I value my house more if I have a right to exclude gasoline stations from the neighborhood.

The cost of exchange is the satisfaction a person has to give up. When someone spends $50 on shoes, the real cost of the shoes is the satisfaction that would be available from another bundle of goods that $50 could buy. By going out on a date the evening before an exam, a student gives up the satisfaction of a higher grade that several hours of additional study could have made possible. In general, the cost of exchange is the value of that which is being given up (i.e., opportunity cost).

In a world of uncertainty and incomplete information, the future consequences of our current decisions can only be anticipated. A pair of shoes might fall apart within a few days, a BMW might turn out to be a lemon, and things might not get better with Coke. Individuals form their own subjective perceptions about future consequences of specific exchange opportunities. Those perceptions are likely to differ from one person to another. Thus, some would choose to negotiate exchanges that other find unattractive.

The Terms and Extent of Exchange

To say that exchange makes us better off does not mean that people carry with them small computers to calculate the increments of satisfaction they expect to derive from each and every exchange. Sometimes we agonize over a decision (e.g., choosing a major), sometimes we act on impulse (e.g., hitting a friend), and sometimes we act out of habit (i.e., buying the same brand of cigars). However, human behavior is consistent in one respect. The bundle of other things that a person is willing to give up in exchange for one unit of a good depends upon preference and income. Given the satisfaction I expect to get from beer, an increase in its price would induce me to drink less beer because the bundle of other things I have to give up is now bigger. That might change when I discover Coors beer.

The importance of income is, however, easy to exaggerate. For example, even though you have $1,000 to spend, you may choose to forgo a second cup of coffee if its price increases from fifty cents to a dollar. The satisfaction you derive from other goods (e.g. beer) that one dollar can buy is the major factor affecting the exchange you choose. Income is primarily a constraint that defines your set of choices.

Suppose an important high-school football game is played in your town. The game is a sellout. Bill was somehow able to get a ticket at the regular price of $20. He is quite happy, because he would have been willing to pay as much as $30 for the ticket; a situation that might change if he were to discover that the new coach of his home team is a poor teacher. But, given his incomplete information, Bill prefers $31 worth of other goods to watching the game. He has four neighbors who are in the same income bracket but differ in the satisfaction they expect to derive from watching the game. Table 7-1 shows the maximum price they are willing pay for tickets.[1]

Table 7-1. The Demand for Tickets

Neighbor 1	$70
Neighbor 2	$60
Neighbor 3	$50
Neighbor 4	$40
Bill	$30

[1] If the team wanted to sell the ticket at the market-clearing price, our analysis would remain the same. As we shall see in chapter 8, high schools may not have incentives to sell tickets to those willing to pay more than others.

Here we have five people who value the same good differently. *They do not know each other's preferences for watching the game.* However, moved by their own desire for more utility, they have incentive to seek exchange. Not knowing Bill's preference for watching the game, neighbor 4 offers $28 for the ticket. Bill turns the offer down because he prefers watching the game to whatever else $28 could buy. However, neighbor 4 has incentives to raise his offer. If and when he offers more than $30, he gets the ticket. Depending on Bill's and neighbor 4's respective bargaining skills (and luck), the price will end up somewhere between $30 and $40. Neighbors 3 and 2 have incentives to raise the offer to $41 and $51 respectively. By raising the offer above $60, say to $64, neighbor 1 will eventually get the ticket. Bill is better off because in exchange for something that to him is worth $30, he gets a bundle of goods worth $64. Neighbor 1 is better off because he gives up a bundle of goods worth $64 in exchange for watching the game that he values at $70. And no one in the community is worse off.

The allocation of the ticket does not depend on prior knowledge of what each person is willing to pay for the opportunity to watch the game. The price of $64 emerges through the choice-making process in a world of incomplete information. By raising their successive offers, those who value the ticket more "bribe" those who value it less to withdraw from competition. Bill ends up with a large profit. However, the price above $60 is necessary in order to allocate the ticket (a scarce good) to a person who values watching the game most.

Since knowledge of other people's utility functions is not available to a decision maker[1], the ticket might change hands several times on its journey to the highest bidder. For example, the outcome would have been the same if neighbor 4 had been able to purchase the ticket from Bill for, say, $36. Neighbor 3 would then bid the ticket away from him for any price in excess of $50, and so on.

---

[1] *Assumptions such as "given" relative prices and/or "given" utility functions are misleading. Those variables do not exist independently from the action-choosing process through which they are generated.*

Neighbor 1 would still get the ticket, but the gains from trade would be shared by several people.

In either case, the ticket is allocated to the highest bidder. All known exchange opportunities are exploited and the extent of exchange is maximized (the allocation of resources is efficient). There is no additional exchange that could make some people better off without making others worse off. Moreover, the value that each of them attaches to watching the game is based on their respective subjective perceptions of the benefits. The competitive process being a knowledge-creating process, those benefits are subject to revisions from one game to another. Their knowledge about each other's preference for watching the game is then likely to remain incomplete.

The Law of Demand

Clearly an inverse relationship exists between the price of a good and the quantity of that good demanded. This proposition is known as the law of demand. The law of demand captures the essence of human behavior in a world of scarcity: people demand more of any good at a lower price and less of that good at a higher price. The law of demand then is one of the most important concepts in economic analysis.

The explanatory and predictive powers of the law of demand arise from its verifiability. A car dealer gives you a better discount when the lot is full of cars for sale. Fresh fruits costs less in season than out of season. When a retail store wants to move some merchandize faster, the manager advertises a lower price. Students have fewer dates the evening before a major exam than the day after. An increase in the price of crime (i.e., the joint probability of getting caught, being convicted, and kept in jail) reduces the rate of criminal activity. At a higher price for shoes, we wear them longer. At a higher price of gasoline, we make fewer trips and eventually look for a smaller car.[1]

Some people claim that there are exceptions from the law of demand. The fact that it takes time to find examples that are not consistent with the law of demand confirms its general validity, however. Economic analysis is more concerned with what we routinely observe than with things that are possible. At any rate, what is the purpose of seeking an exception from the behavior that we constantly observe?

The Demand Schedule

Let us return to our example. The demand schedule for football tickets is summarized in Table 7-2.

Table 7-2. Five-Person Demand for Tickets

Price	Bill	N'bor 1	N'bor 2	N'bor 3	N'bor 4	Total
>70	0	0	0	0	1	1
>60	0	0	0	1	1	2
>50	0	0	1	1	1	3
>40	0	1	1	1	1	4
>30	1	1	1	1	1	5

[1] Adjustments to changes in the variables that affect costs and benefits of using a good are always costly. The more time we have to make adjustments, the lower is the cost of making efficient adjustments. In price theory we summarize this by saying that the demand of any good tends to get more elastic in the long run.

We can use information in Table 7-2 to draw a standard diagram on the demand schedule for tickets by plotting quantities demanded against prices. The demand schedule shows the quantity of a good that is demanded per unit of time or activity (e.g., football game), all other things such as property rights, preferences, incomes, and prices of other goods being given.[1] However, while the law of demand is a general proposition that accurately describes human behavior, the demand schedule for a good attempts to provide specific information on how much of that good is going to be bought at each given price. Given the cost of information as well as the continuous knowledge-creating process of market competition, all that we really know about the demand schedule for any specific good is that more of that good is bought at lower than at higher prices. Even if we were able to learn what the demand schedule of a good actually is, we would have only learned what it was.

The demand schedule of a good is always drawn sloping down to the right. Because its slopes conform to the law of demand, it has become one of the most useful tools in economic analysis.

PRODUCTION

To produce one unit of any good we have to use a bundle of other goods. It is customary to refer to the goods required to produce other goods as resources.[2] Like all other goods, resources have alternative uses. The cost of producing one unit of any good then is the market

[1] The effect of changes in those factors is to shift the demand schedule in one or the other direction. For example, making nontransferable a currently transferable property right to cut a given quantity of trees in a public forest would reduce the price of that right.

[2] The book uses those two terms interchangeably.

value of other goods the same bundle of resources could have produced in the same time period.[1]

Neoclassical theory says that production is technically efficient when the output of any good cannot be increased without reducing the output of some other good. This definition implies that decisions are made in an institutional vacuum. Each good is produced by the lowest-cost producer of that good and each additional bundle of supplies of that good is produced by successively higher-cost producers, period. But transaction costs are part of the total cost of production. Moreover, transaction costs are not invariant with respect to changes and modifications in the rules of the game, meaning that institutional structures affect efficiency in production.

Private Property Rights and Production

Suppose that five entrepreneurs are producing video cassette recorders. Table 7-3 shows the quantity of VCRs that each can produce per unit of time, and their opportunity costs in terms of the market value of alternative outputs that have to be given up. The costs of producing VCRs thus include the payments that each producer has to make for the right to use resources that belong to other people (labor, parts, glass, etc.), as well as the value of their own resources in alternative uses.

In a private property economy, no entrepreneur among the five would choose to produce VCRs at any price below $30. They all do better for themselves by producing something else. If and when the price per VCR rises above $30, C would, driven by his desire for more, switch from whatever he was doing to making VCRs. His decision benefits the community as well. At $32 per VCR, C makes a profit of $2 per VCR, while the community gives up $30 worth of other goods in exchange for a VCR which it values at $32.

---

[1] The statement applies to all scarce goods. The costs of making Charlie into a good friend are my time (that is, alternative activities I would also have enjoyed) and the money I spend going out with him.

Table 7-3. Five Person Production Alternatives

Persons	VCR in units	$ of Alter. Goods	Cost per VCR
A	250	27,500	$110
B	300	27,000	$90
C	100	3,000	$30
D	200	14,000	$70
E	400	20,000	$50

It is clear that $30 per VCR is the minimum price at which C could produce VCRs, $50 is the minimum price for E, and so on. The result of this interaction between the right of ownership and the desire for more satisfaction produces a supply schedule. The right of ownership creates incentives for the supply schedule to slope upward to the right. It shows the minimum price necessary to encourage producers to offer each given quantity of that good for sale. The upward slope of the supply schedule indicates that production is technically efficient. If E were the first to produce VCRs, the community would have wasted $20 worth of other goods per one VCR.

OBSTACLES TO EXCHANGE AND PRODUCTION

Neoclassical equilibrium represents a situation where all exchange and/or production opportunities have been exploited, where no individuals find it to their advantage to seek to change the set of contractual bargains (the maximization paradigm), and where, consequently, the allocation of resources is efficient. However, the world is full of observations that cast doubts on both the existence and the usefulness of the concept of equilibrium. By ignoring the effects of institutional structures and transaction costs on the terms and extent of exchange, the maximization paradigm tells us little about real world processes.

Transaction Costs.

Suppose neighbor 1 lives across town. He might never learn about the availability of a ticket at a price he is willing to pay; hence neighbor 2 might end up watching the game. Entrepreneur C might never know that VCRs are being sold at a price above $30 in another marketing area. When I build my house in Texas I might be giving up a higher-valued use for land (drilling for oil). Positive transaction costs prevent resources from ending up in their more valuable uses.

In a private property economy, people have incentives to seek new exchange opportunities as well as to modify existing ones. This means that exchange opportunities are not "given"; thus, they cannot be maximized. People have incentives to seek ways to reduce transaction costs, which means that transaction costs are not "given" either. In short, new opportunities for exchange are continuously created and transaction costs continuously lowered in the choice-making process. Scalpers, retail merchants, advertising agencies, real estate companies and employment bureaus among others, continuously seek to reduce transaction costs. And they bear the cost of their efforts whenever the gains from additional exchange, which they make possible, turn out to be less than the reduction in transaction costs. An unintended efficiency-enhancing consequence of this process is that resources tend to move from less to more valuable uses.

The right of ownership also creates incentives for transaction costs to be reduced by those who can do this at a lower cost. Sometimes it is the seller and sometimes it is the buyer. For example, the attributes of many goods are costly to measure. I want to buy oranges to make fresh juice but I do not know which oranges are good for juice and which are better for eating. Or, after a long drive through the state of Montana, I am looking for a comfortable bed in a clean room. Or I want to buy a VCR but my neighbor tells me about problems he has with his new unit. So am I going to end up choosing less valuable alternatives such as buying frozen juice, renting a VCR, and sleeping in a motel with a nice exterior and dirty rooms? Not necessarily.

Producers of oranges can separate them by quality at a lower cost than I can. And the right of ownership gives them incentives to do that. A motel owner knows that the greater the variability in quality of rooms of average price in the motel industry as a whole, the more valuable is information about the rooms in a particular motel. Out of his own self-interest, the motel owner might associate with a chain that has a widely known set of standards. When I see a sign for Ramada Inn I know, with a small variance, what to expect. A hotel down the road could be both better and cheaper, but the cost of driving around to purchase additional information about the quality of independent motels could be quite high relative to the certainty of checking into a brand-name establishment.

In the case of many durable goods, the cost of measuring the variability of quality around the average value is reduced as the goods are used. The buyer is then a cheaper provider of information about the attributes of cars, VCRs, television sets, and many other durable goods. By offering customers all kinds of warranties, guarantees and return privileges, the seller reduces transaction costs by shifting the quality control to them.

Nonpecuniary Goods.

We observe that some exchange and production opportunities are not exploited even though their transaction costs are low. It is wrong to interpret those cases as the failure of private property rights to move resources to their higher-valued uses. People derive satisfaction from a number of specific "goods" such as a pleasant environment, congenial colleagues, friendly neighbors, and clean air. Those are scarce goods; that is, we purchase them at a price. I might prefer Dallas to New York, humble colleagues in a second-rate academic department to self-centered scholars is a great department, an ethnic neighborhood to a mixed neighborhood, and fresh country air in College Station to the air in Los Angeles.

The satisfaction we derive from nonpecuniary goods has its pecuniary income equivalent. An additional $5,000 per year would not make me move from Dallas to New York. But $50,000 would. Or suppose I own a house with an apartment to rent. A widow with five children offers to pay $500 per month for that apartment, while a plumber offers $450. I might decide that to have a friendly plumber around is worth more to me than $50 per month. But for $600 per month the widow with kids could get the apartment. The satisfaction we receive from purchasing specific "goods" is subjective and has its money income equivalent.

Charitable giving is also a source of satisfaction. When I give $10 to the boy scouts I am saying that the satisfaction I derive from that exchange is more important to me than whatever satisfaction I could get from another bundle of goods that $10 could buy. The fact that we discriminate in making contributions is evidence that they are made in the pursuit of our self-interest. We give to those people and institutions whose happiness is important to us. Charitable giving also conforms to the law of demand. A tax reduction makes charitable giving more expensive and people give less.

PRIVATE PROPERTY RIGHTS AND PRICE COMPETITION

The demand schedule is not known to those who buy and sell goods. The same goes for the supply schedule. As we have seen, this knowledge is not necessary in a private property economy. The right of ownership provides strong incentives for buyers and producers continuously to seek ways to reduce transaction costs and move their resources to higher-valued uses. The competitive process is thus a knowledge-creating process which continuously and incrementally modifies the subjective perceptions individuals have about their sets of choices and trade-offs.

Data in Table 7-4 are hypothetical and conform to both the law of demand and the incentives effects of private property rights.

They illustrate two critical functions of relative prices: to allocate the supply of a good among competing users (who gets what), and to control changes in the supply of that good (who should produce what). In that sense data in Table 7-4 help us to understand the *tendencies* inherent in the choice-making process in a private-property, free-market economy. It is important, however, to bear in mind that the tendencies could only tell us what the equilibrium would have been if those tendencies continued to work during the period of observation and if no other factors (including new knowledge) intervened. And that is never the case. The properties of the equilibrium-to-be change with changes in knowledge and other factors that influence our subjective perceptions of reality. And we know that changes in knowledge and those other factors depend on institutional structures and transaction costs. They are not exogenous constraints of neoclassical theory.

Suppose that the price per VCR is $21 and no VCRs are produced. At that price a number of people prefer VCRs to whatever else $21 could buy. Whether they offer to pay more for VCRs or some producers raise the price in response to observed shortages of VCRs is irrelevant. What is important is that the price is going to be bid up. As the price is bid to $31 per VCR, two things happen. First, C finds it in his self-interest to produce VCRs. The desire for more satisfaction plus the right to keep the benefits from making VCRs (a component of the right of ownership) provide C with sufficient incentives to respond to the demand for that good at any price above $30. Second, as the price per VCR goes up, some people decide that a VCR is not worth a larger bundle of other things that has to be sacrificed, and switch to other goods. The process of bidding higher the price then reduces the shortage of VCRs.

As the price is bid up to $50, C makes more profit but no additional VCRs reach the market. However, this increase in the price per VCR is necessary for two reasons. First, it helps to induce some people, who like VCRs but not as much as some others do, to drop out of the market (or buy fewer units). Second, an increase in price is necessary to bring in higher-cost producers of VCRs.

At the price of $51, E finds it in her self-interest to begin producing VCRs. She does not know the market demand schedule for

Table 7-4. Demand and Supply of VCRs

Price in $	Demand for VCRs	Supply of VCRs
141	140	1,250
131	160	1,250
121	180	1,250
111	200	1,250
101	220	1,000
91	240	1,000
81	260	700
71	280	700
61	300	500
51	320	500
41	340	100
31	360	100
21	380	0

VCRs. If she jumps in with both feet and makes only VCRs, the total supply of VCRs (made by C plus E) would increase to 500. At $51 per unit, people are willing to buy only 320 units. E discovers that she cannot sell all that she has produced. She has to stop making VCRs and try to sell her unanticipated inventory of them below the costs of production, or take time to work inventories down, or go bankrupt. As her inventories are depleted, E learns that while she cannot sell 400 VCRs at a profit, she might increase her total earnings by selling some units. Suppose that by trial and error, she ends up producing 200 VCRs. The price at which C and E sell the supply of 300 VCRs is $61. C gets rich and E does well, too. Her total revenue is now $22,200 ($12,200 from selling 200 VCRs at $61, and $10,000 from using the rest of her resources to produce other goods), which is better than the $20,000 she made before switching to VCRs.

Yet, E has incentives to sell additional VCRs at any price above $50 provided that those sales have no effect on the price ($61) at which she sells the first 200 units. Indeed, we observe a number of methods used to reduce transaction costs of negotiating additional exchanges without a reduction in the prevailing market price, such as buying two units of a good at a discount (one suit for $500, two for $650), tie-in sales (50% discount on oil changes for five years when you buy a Honda at Bob's Place), and all sorts of bonuses (American Advantage program).

Analogously, the same process of searching for, discovering, and negotiating exchange opportunities takes place when the quantity demanded exceeds the quantity supplied.

To conclude, the right of ownership and contractual freedom create incentives for individuals (i) spontaneously to negotiate contractual agreements that move resources to their higher-valued uses, (ii) spontaneously to seek new opportunities for exchange and production, and (iii) spontaneously to seek ways to reduce transaction costs. Does this mean that a private property economy is always or sometimes or ever efficient? Economic analysis cannot tell us that. However, economic analysis tells us that the right of ownership and contractual freedom provide incentives for individuals to keep increasing the extent of exchange.

It is in that sense--the effects of its institutions on the direction of economic activity--that capitalism is an efficient system.[1]

---

[1] That is why I do not here postulate the objective of maximizing the extent of exchange (and/or production).

THE ROLE OF PROFIT

The high cost of information, positive transaction costs, and various property rights impede the transfer of resources in the direction of greater efficiency. Yet, every society must tackle the problems of identifying the best uses for resources and transferring resources from lower- to higher-valued uses. Some sort of authority is expected to look after those problems in a socialist state. In capitalism, profit performs this function.

Profits are earnings per period of time in excess of the opportunity costs of resources used in production. Suppose the interest on government bonds is 8 percent. If a business in which you invested $1,000 gives you $60 per year after all direct costs are paid, you lost $20. The cost of investing $1,000 in that business must include the $80 you could have obtained by investing in government bonds. If the business yields $90 after direct costs are paid, your profit is $10. In other words profit is the amount over and above what a resource could earn in the best alternative use adjusted for risks (that is why the rate of interest on government bonds is usually used as a measure of the best alternative). In a private property economy, those annual profits can be taken out in one lamp sum by selling the assets that generated them. The value of the asset is the expected stream of profits discounted at the market rate of interest.

In a private property economy, changes in profits provide quick, reliable and low-cost information about changes in relative prices and preferences. For example, suppose that people shift their preference between hamburgers and pizza in favor of the latter. The demand for pizza would increase relative to the demand for hamburgers. The resulting change in relative prices of pizza and hamburgers would affect profit rates in those two industries. The rate of return on one dollar worth of resources in the pizza industry would increase relative to the rate of return in the hamburger industry. The owners of resources have incentives to respond to this information by transferring their assets from lower-valued uses (hamburgers) to higher-valued uses (pizza).[1]

Positive profits in the pizza industry would eventually be whittled away through competition that lowers the price of pizza (larger supplies) and raises the value of resources used in the production of pizza. However, other things continuously happen in the economy. The transfer of resources to higher-valued uses generates the demand for knowledge *specific* to new exchange opportunities. The competitive process then creates, modifies and changes knowledge. We observe the consequences of those changes in knowledge as innovations (and their subsequent imitations) in lower transaction costs of making pizza (e.g. mobile vans), new types of pizza (e.g. low fat pizza), new methods of baking pizza (pre-packaging), and new ingredients for pizza.

The social forces that govern this never ending process of producing and diffusing new knowledge as well as their economic implications, rather than the properties of the equilibrium with zero profit, explain the working of the private-property, free-market economy.

James Buchanan: "ASYMMETRICAL RECIPROCITY IN MARKET EXCHANGE: IMPLICATIONS FOR ECONOMIES IN TRANSITION"[2]

Introduction

---

[1] If and when higher profits are taxed away as windfall gains, the owners of assets earning those profits must lose incentives to respond to changes in individuals' preferences. Limitations on profit rates obstruct the vital allocative function they perform in guiding the allocation of resources.

[2] **Social Philosophy & Policy**, 10. Summer 1993. Copyright Social Philosophy and Policy Foundation. Reprinted with the permission of Cambridge University Press and author.

Western visitors to those parts of the world that before 1991 were politically organized as the Soviet Union have been impressed by the attitudes of persons toward behavior in ordinary exchanges, attitudes that seem to be so different from those in Western economies. The essential element of an "exchange culture" seem to be missing, and this absence, in itself, may be central to the effective functioning of market economies.[1] Individual participants in ordinary exchange relationships in Western Economies act as if they understand the simplest of all economic principles, namely, that there are mutual gains from trade, that the benefits are reciprocal, that exchange is a positive-sum game. This "as if" understanding, which remains perhaps below our level of consciousness in the West, is largely missing from the public attitudes of citizens of the former Soviet Union, who behave as if the gains from trade do not exist, or at least are one-sided rather than mutual.

There is a familiar story that illustrates the thesis: "In the Soviet Union, both party to an exchange lose; one party loses the goods; the other party loses the money." This statement may offer a concise, if exaggerated, summary of the general attitude toward exchange that seems to describe the behavior of many (of course, not all) persons in the republics that were formerly parts of the Soviet Union.

In this essay, I propose to offer an economic explanation for some of the differences in behavioral attitudes that we observe, as between Western economies and those of the Eurasian republics. In the West, with developed market systems, economists concentrate initial attention on the mutuality of trading gains and on the reciprocity in any exchange relationship. And a recognition of this reciprocity seems to inform public participation in markets. What is often overlooked is the asymmetry in the reciprocal relationship between buyer and seller in developed money economies. The buyer

---

[1] See James Buchanan, "Tacit Presuppositions of Political Economy: Implications for Societies in Transition" (George Mason University, Fairfax, VA: Center for Study of Public Choice, 1991), mimeograph. The present essay builds on, extends, and modifies the argument of this earlier paper.

of goods and/or services who offers, or "sells," money in exchange processes possesses a bargaining advantage that is often overlooked. The central-command economy reverses the direction of advantage, even when exchange dealings are permitted. The differences in the incentives that confront participants in the two organizational settings generate predictable differences in observed behavior and in behavioral attitudes.

I should stress at the outset that my focus is exclusively on the economic, as opposed to the ideological sources of explanation of observed behavior in the exchange process. The ideological denigration of market exchange, as a general system of organizing economic relationships, may have exerted influences on individual behavior over and beyond those analyzed here. And, of course, at some higher system level where organizational-institutional decisions on structure were made, ideological motivation may explain why persons were confronted with circumstances that contain divergent economic incentives.

Idealized Exchange--A Pure Barter Economy

Consider a setting in which the exchange process operates ideally, in the analytical-conceptual sense and beyond any feasibility limits imposed by the limits of human capacities. Persons enter into exchange dealings, one with another, in the full knowledge of all potential trading opportunities. Further, the exchange network, the economy, is sufficiently large such that, for each and every buyer or seller in the market for each and every good and service, input or output, there exist large numbers of sellers or buyers, among whom any single buyer or seller may choose. Finally, there are no costs incurred by any buyer or seller in shifting from one alternative to another.

Note that, in such an idealized, zero-transaction-cost setting, no person, whether buyer or seller, in any exchange relationship secures any differential gain from exchanging with the single seller or buyer with whom a particular exchange is effectuated. Neither's party action, in making the particular cross market transfer, generates benefits for the other, for the simple reasons that alternative buyers and sellers, to whom trade may be shifted, are available at no cost. Gain emerges, of course, to any person, whether buyer or seller, from the availability of or access to "the market," without which grossly inefficient self-production would be necessary.

For my purpose, the noteworthy feature of this idealized model is the implied behavioral indifference that each participant in the exchange network will exhibit toward those with whom exchanges are made. In such a setting, nothing that might be called an "exchange culture" would have meaning. Each participant may, if he or she chooses, behave as if he or she exists in total independence of others, despite the complete interdependence among all persons who participate in the inclusive network. No buyer need invest any effort in persuading, cajoling, or convincing any seller to offer goods and services, and no seller, similarly, will find it rational to try to persuade any buyer to take his wares off the shelf. The reason is straightforward: there exists a sufficiently large number of alternative sellers or buyers to insure that, if one person does not trade, a replacement immediately appears to whom trade can be shifted and at no differential cost.

Idealized Exchange with Money

I now propose to modify the idealized exchange model described in section II in only one respect. Assume, as before, that there are no costs of making exchanges, and that all participants have full knowledge about the qualities of goods. Further, assume, again as before, that the economy is large, and that there are many sellers and many buyers in the market for each good and service. Assume now, however, that there are limits to the knowledge that any participant has about the location of those persons in the economy who seek to purchase precisely the same good he or she seeks to sell, and vice versa. That is to say, direct barter is costly in the sense that each participant in a potential trade must undergo some search effort in locating the desired matching trading partner.

Recognition of the costs of search that make direct barter inefficient provides an economic explanation for the emergence of money, either in the form of some good that comes to be widely accepted as a medium of general exchange through some process of cultural evolution, or in the form of some good or some symbolic representation, the value of which is guaranteed by the collective body that protects private property, that is, by the state. The existence of money allows sellers to eliminate costly searches for other persons who are themselves sellers of goods that are desired in exchange. Similarly, money allows buyers to purchase goods that they desire without the necessity of searching for persons who seek to buy precisely that which they offer in exchange as sellers. The familiar metaphor that refers to money as the lubricant of the exchange system is helpfully explanatory.

Under the severely restrictive conditions assumed to exist, however, the behaviorally relevant conclusion reached above with reference to the idealized exchange economy seem to continue to hold. Since there are many buyers and many sellers in the markets for any good or service, any input or output, the individual participant need not be at all concerned about the person with whom an exchange is effectuated. The seller of red shoes need not invest in efforts to convince potential buyers to purchase his stocks since, by definition, there exist alternative buyers who will purchase the stocks and with no cost to the seller. Similarly, the buyer of red apples need not invest in attempts to persuade any single apple seller to offer his wares, since, again by definition, there exist many alternative apple sellers to whom the apple buyer may turn and without cost. There is no economic basis for the emergence of any attitude other than behavioral indifference toward specifically identified cross-exchange partners.

Asymmetrical Reciprocity

The asymmetry enters when we recognize that the money side of any exchange has an inherent "transaction costs" advantage, which in turn improves the "bargaining" power of the person who takes such a role. Consider, once again, a pure barter economy without money, but with some limits on knowledge. Clearly, the person who possesses or produces a good that is, relatively, more generally desired that others will find it less costly to effectuate exchanges for whatever goods he ultimately desires. Money becomes the limiting case of a good that is generally desired by all participants in the exchange network, even if not intrinsically but instrumentally. The trader who accepts money for units of any non-money good or service secures a nonspecific medium of value that facilitates reentry into any market. The ideal fungibility of money gives the supplier-seller of money an asymmetrical claim to the gains from exchange. By the very definition of what money is, the possessor, and hence potential supplier, of money faces lower transaction costs in completing and exchange than the possessor, and potential supplier, of any nonmoney good or service. The fungibility of money provides the possessor with enhanced power to "walk away" from any exchange for goods and services, a power that the possessor of any nonmoney good or service simply does not have.

The basic asymmetry in the money-goods exchange is obscured by the proclivity of economic theorists to "define away" the features of the exchange process that are sometimes of most interest. As noted, if transaction costs were, literally, defined away, there would be no need for money at all; the pure barter economy would operate with ideal efficiency. When the rigorous assumptions required for the working of a pure barter economy are modified, however, and money is recognized to be an efficiency-enhancing institution, attempts are made to idealize the operation of the money economy by postulating that each and every buyer and seller, whether of goods or money, faces a sufficiently large number of cross-exchange options to guarantee that no person has market or exchange power, in the differential sense instanced above. Once transaction costs are introduced at all, however, there seems to be no plausibly acceptable logic for refusing to acknowledge differential in "bargaining" advantages as between those persons who enter markets as supplier-sellers of money and those who enter as demanders-buyers. To put the same proposition conversely, it is the demanders-buyers of goods and services that have an asymmetrical advantage over the suppliers-sellers, and in all markets.

As we move away from the abstract models for the working of a production-exchange economy and toward a more-descriptively satisfying appreciation of the economy as it actually seems to function, the basic asymmetry identified here may become painfully obvious, and my whole discussion may be taken to represent trituration. I suggest, however, that the money-goods asymmetry assists in an understanding of much of the behavior that we observe in developing countries, both historically and currently. The institutions of market exchange, as we know them, incorporate a recognition of this asymmetry, even to the extent that their familiarity breeds analytical oversight.

In markets as we know them, sellers of goods and services peddle their wares, advertise, create attractive displays, adopt attitudes of differential demeanor toward potential buyers, and behave, generally, as if their customers' interests are their own. "We aim to please"-this slogan describes the attitudes of those traders on the goods-and-services side of the goods-money exchanges, rather than vice versa. And we should find ourselves surprised if this behavior were absent. We do not observe buyers of goods and services setting up their own market stalls with signs that read "we buy apples," except in unusual circumstances. In product markets, we see some, but not much, buyer advertising. Potential buyers of goods and services apparently feel under no compulsion to act as if the interests of a seller are of relevance. Such buyers remain behaviorally indifferent toward the interests of any identified seller.[1]

---

[1] Labor markets may seem to offer an exception to the generalizations suggested here. Sellers of labor (a service) sometimes advertise their availability, but more often it is buyers of labor (employers) who advertise to attract sellers. The absence of

The distinction between the two sides of the money-goods exchange stressed here does not depend on the pricing institutions that are in place. In developed economies, sellers tend to offer their wares to potential buyers at quasi-fixed prices, and the latter remain free to purchase varying quantities. In many developing economies, by contrast, sellers do not fix prices in advance, save as some preliminary move in what becomes a complex bargaining game with buyers. In both sets of pricing arrangements, however, we observe sellers-suppliers in the active role of seekers for potential buyers and investors in efforts at persuasion, rather than the opposite.

The asymmetry stressed here is, of course, implicitly recognized in the usage of the term "consumers' sovereignty" to describe the exchange economy. This term, which might be better replaced by "buyers' sovereignty," suggests that sellers of goods and services, or suppliers, are and must be responsive to the interests of buyers, and, hence, that the latter are the ultimate sources of evaluation. Conventional discussion of the consumers' sovereignty feature of market economies does not, however, take much note of the relevant behavioral implications.

An alternative way of discussing the asymmetry in the money-goods exchange relationship is to introduce the differential specificity of valued assets, as held by each party prior to exchange. Whether we analyze a pure exchange economy, in which persons commence with determinate endowments of goods, or a production-exchange economy, in which persons commence with endowments of talents that may be organized to produce goods, the potential supplier in any exchange for money is, by definition, locked in, relatively, by the specificity of the valued asset in possession, pre-exchange, and, for this reason, is more vulnerable to terms-of-trade manipulation than the potential cross-

homogeneity among separate units demanded (that is, the variation in skills and qualifications among potential employees) may offset, or even reverse, the direction of effect emphasized here generally.

exchange demander, whose pre-exchange valued asset takes the form of money.[1]

Asymmetry Inversion in Command Economy

How would it be possible to remove or even to reverse the asymmetry in the basic exchange relationship in an economy? Reversion to a system of barter through some prohibition of a generalized money medium could remove the asymmetry here, but only at the expense of gross inefficiencies occasioned by the costs of search. In such an economy-one without money but with transaction costs-each market participant is both a buyer and a seller of goods, and there is no generalized advantage to either side of an exchange. As noted earlier, there would be a particularized advantage to either the buyer or seller of the goods that are in relatively wider usage in the economy.

Let us consider, now, an economy in which money has been introduced, but where money is not, in itself, a sufficient medium to insure the effectuation of an exchange. Such an economy would be described by money prices for goods, but accompanied by some set of complementary nonmonetary "prices", or arrangements, that would be required to complete a transaction. The nominal money prices for goods and services would be politically established--and at a level below those prices that would clear markets, that would equate demand and supply. Straightforward public-choice analysis of the incentives of persons in bureaucratic authority to set money prices suggests that such prices will remain always below market-clearing

---

[1] This relationship between differential assets specificity as between parties to contract, and the vulnerability to opportunistic behavior, has been discussed by Armen Alchian and Susan Woodward, "Reflections on the Theory of the Firm," Journal of Institutional and Theoretical Economics, 143, no. 1 (1987), pp. 110-37. More generally, economists have analyzed the effects of asymmetric information in the operation of exchange. The pioneer in these efforts was Akerlof, G. "The Market for Lemons': Quality Uncertainty and Market Mechanism," Quarterly Journal of Economics, 84 (August 1970), pp. 488-500.

levels.[1] Bureaucrats lose any rationing authority if prices are set at market-clearing levels, and such authority is desired both for its own sake and as a source for the extraction of favors (rents). There will tend to exist excess demands for the supplies of goods brought forth in all markets. Each seller will tend to face more demanders for his product that can possibly be satisfied.

In such a setting, any reason that a seller-supplier might have for acting as if he is motivated by the interests of buyers is absent. Sellers will be behaviorally indifferent toward each and all potential buyers; they will have no incentive to please particular buyers, not even to the extent of providing quality merchandise, since there will always be buyers ready and willing to purchase whatever is made available to them.

Consider, by contrast, the behavioral stance of the participant who enters the exchange relationship as a potential buyer, who possesses a stock of money in the hope of securing goods and services. Each person in such a role will face the frustration experienced in an inability to get the goods in the quantities desired, and of the quality standards wanted. Buyers, with money, become the residual claimants to the gains from exchange, a role that is directly contrary to that which buyers occupy in the well-functioning money economy, as analyzed earlier. "Buyers' sovereignty," which was mentioned earlier as a shorthand description of the central feature of the exchange economy, is replaced by "sellers' sovereignty," provided we are careful to include within the "sellers" category those persons who hold bureaucratic authority to establish arrangements for nonprice rationing among demanders of goods and services.

In the command economy, as sketched out in capsule here, buyers of goods and services become the supplicants, who must curry favor with the seller and their agents, who must, somehow, "aim to please," over and beyond some mere offer of generalized purchasing power in the form of money. Sellers remain indifferent to the pleas of buyers, and not only because of the excess number of demanders.

---

[1] David Levy, "The Bias in Centrally Planned Prices," Public Choice, 67, no. 3 (December 1990), pp. 213-26.

Sellers also realize that if they exchange goods for money, they, too, must return to other markets as buyers, who must, in turn, expect to encounter the frustrations of buyers throughout the system.

The chronic "shortage" of goods that describes the workings of the command economy stems directly from the imposed politicization of money prices, as does the generalized supplication of buyers toward sellers-suppliers, including the relevant members of the bureaucratic apparatus. The institution of money, as such, is not allowed to serve its standard efficiency-enhancing function. The nonprice rationing arrangements, which emerge as supplementary to money prices, become analogous, in their economic effects, to the search costs that barter involves in the absence of money.

The command economy, with politicized money prices, along with supplementary rationing arrangements, will be characterized by a "money overhang," that is, by a supply of money that is in excess of that which is needed in exchange transactions, at the politically set money prices. Indeed, without such "money overhand" the authority that is exercised by the whole price central regime loses its "bite." Unless potential consumers-buyers are provided with more money (through wage payments) than they can spend on products, at the controlled prices, the authority of bureaucrats to ration scarce supplies becomes unnecessary. This excess money supply, in its turn, sets up additional incentives for the emergence of exchange transactions that are outside the boundaries of legitimacy in some formal sense. Black, shadow, or underground markets will emerge more readily when persons are unable to satisfy their demands for goods through standard exchange channels and when they have available, at the same time, unused and unusable stocks of money. As this shadow sector increases in size over time, as measured either by the volume of transactions or by the number of participants, the behavioral norms that describe the operation of the whole legal order must be undermined.

The fact that money is not allowed fully to perform its efficiency-enhancing role in the economy must also set in motion evolutionary pressures toward the emergence of some good that will secure general acceptability as "real money," quit distinct from the money issued by the state monopoly. In Russia, and in other former socialist economies, the currency of developed nations has emerged to fill this role, at least in part. And, in the shadow exchanges between these monies and goods, the asymmetry observed in Western economies is partially restored. Sellers of goods do, indeed, seek out and court potential buyers who are thought to possess hard currencies.

This transitional stage aside, however, the point to be emphasized is that, in the command economy, as it traditionally functions, the whole economic culture is dramatically different from that which we observe in Western market economies. The near-total absence of seller-supplier efforts to attract and to please potential buyers shocks Western observers who visit the territories of the former Soviet Union. The paucity of billboards in the Moscow of 1990 was not primarily attributable to regulatory prohibition. The result emerged directly from the fact that no seller-supplier of any good or service felt any economic pressure to respond to customer interests or to expand the demands for products. The sales clerk at the kiosk, as a selling agent, behaved very differently from her Western counterpart, but not because of ethnic origins; she behaved differently because in the Russian mindset that permeates the citizenry generally, the seller-purveyor of goods need not be concerned about customers.

The Russian visitor to the United State is equally surprised when the behavior of sellers-suppliers is observed, both directly and indirectly. Such a visitor is overwhelmed by the neon blazes, the multicolored billboards, the slick magazine pages, and the TV commercials, as well as behaviorally by the stance of those persons who act as agents for suppliers for almost all goods and services. Coming out of an economic culture where buyers are the universal supplicants, the Russian visitor stands aghast at the supplication of sellers and their agents. Neither this Russian visitor nor his American counterpart in Moscow understands that the dramatic differences in the two cultures can be explained, at least in large part, by variations in the incentive structures. The American setting allows the asymmetry in the money-goods exchange relationship to be played out fully in the development and operation of its market institutions. The Soviet Union, by contrast, attempted, throughout its existence, to counter this asymmetry by the politicization of money prices, with an acknowledged major increase in the costs of making transactions, but also with the unrecognized impetus given to the emergence and operation of an economic culture that must be subversive in any effort to move toward the market structure.

SUGGESTED READING

Alchian, A. and Allen, W. Exchange and Production, Belmont: Wadsworth Publishing Co, 1983, chapters 3-5

Ferguson, C. The Neoclassical Theory of Production and Distribution, Cambridge: Cambridge University Press, 1969, chapters 1-6.

Posner, R. Economic Analysis of Law, Boston: Little, Brown and Co, 1992, chapters 2 and 4.

Chapter 8

RESTRICTIONS ON PRIVATE PROPERTY RIGHTS, EXCHANGE, AND PRODUCTION

The government does not have to say: "There shall be price competition." Price competition simply happens whenever the right of ownership and contractual freedom are enforced. As discussed in the previous chapter, the right of ownership and contractual freedom provide incentives for individuals to pursue activities that have the unintended consequence of moving resources from lower- to higher-valued uses. Transaction costs interfere with the efficiency of price competition, and the demand for nonpecuniary goods is frequently confused with inefficient behaviors. The right of ownership and contractual freedom provide strong incentives for individuals to seek ways to increase the extent of exchange via reduction in transaction costs.

This chapter discusses the effects of some specific restrictions on private property rights and contractual freedom that are frequently observed in capitalist economies.

PRICE CONTROLS

Suppose that the government decides to impose a ceiling on the price of a good. In that case, the government attenuates (weakens) the right of ownership by interfering with the owner's right to transfer that good to another individual at a mutually agreed upon price. A major consequence of price controls, then, is to eliminate price competition as a method for resolving the issue of who gets what.

If the maximum price per football ticket in the case discussed earlier is set at $35 (and the school continues to sell tickets at $20), the quantity demanded would be four tickets and the quantity supplied would be one. By selling his ticket at $35, Bill is better off.

He exchanges watching the game that is worth $30 to him for a bundle of goods that is worth $35. However, Bill is not as well off as he would have been if he were free to exchange his ticket at a freely negotiated price (remember it was $64). Moreover, Bill is going to fare the same way regardless of who buys the ticket. He has no incentives to seek the highest-valued use for the ticket. If he sold the ticket to neighbor 1, the only effect of price controls would be a change in the distribution of income. Bill would gain less and neighbor 1 would gain more than in our free exchange example.[1] Should Bill choose to trade with any other neighbor, each of them would feel better off because they all value the ticket in excess of $35. However, each of them could reach even a higher level of satisfaction by selling the ticket to neighbor 1. An important consequence of price controls is thus to reduce the extent of exchange or--the same thing--to leave some beneficial exchange opportunities unexploited.

While price controls eliminate price competition as a method for resolving the allocation of goods among competing individuals, they cannot eliminate the fact of scarcity. Thus, a different type of competition has to be used to decide who gets what. To appreciate the consequences of different methods of competition, let us return to the VCR example in Table 7-4.

Suppose the government decides that the price per VCR should not exceed $41.[2] At that price the demand for VCRs (340) exceeds the supply (100). E has no incentive to enter the market, and the shortage of VCRs is going to continue for as long as price controls are maintained. More people can "afford" VCRs but there are only 100 units for sale at the price of $41 per VCR because of E's lack of incentive to make more. The seller could sell the supply of 100 VCRs

---

[1] An important consequence of price controls is that the owner of a good is denied the right to appropriate the full value of the asset. This section of the book asks an important question: what are the costs of weakening private property rights and are they less than expected benefits?

[2] The most frequent justification for price controls is that at a lower price more people could afford the good.

on a first-come, first-served basis. This type of competition discriminates against people who cannot withstand long hours in a queue or who cannot afford time to do that. For example, a student could find it less expensive in terms of other activities to wait in line for VCRs than would a medical doctor who forgoes $400 per hour away from the office. The first-come, first-served method of competition creates two sets of incentives: a black market for VCRs and a market for people whose time is less valuable to wait in line on behalf of those whose time is more valuable.

At the price of $41 per VCRs, the seller has something to give that is hard to get. Although unable to accept more money for VCRs, the seller can, without breaking the rule, trade favors: the seller has incentives to allocate VCRs to individuals who offer favors in return. A car dealer, a physician, a plumber, an attractive member of the opposite sex and the person in charge of selling tickets for high-school football games are likely to have more favors to trade than a student or a retiree. Indeed, we observed this type of allocation during the shortage of oil caused by price controls in 1973-74.

Minimum wage laws are another form of price controls. They restrict the worker's property right to seek exchange opportunities for labor below some minimum wage. By prohibiting producers from paying their employees less than the legal minimum wage per hour, these laws create unemployment among the least skilled workers. The hardest hit groups are teenagers, African-Americans, women, and the aged. As an alternative to welfare, minimum wage laws create incentives for unemployed workers to seek "contracts across markets"; instead of driving a taxi for less than the minimum wage, one might rent a cab from the company. The purpose of minimum wage laws is that everybody should make a "decent" wage. Unfortunately, there is always a gap between the intent and the observed consequences of exogenous changes in the rules of the game. Evidence is conclusive that minimum wage laws, like all other forms of price controls, tend to hurt precisely those they are supposed to help. A justification for restricting one's property rights in one's labor is that the cost of welfare payments to workers who cannot find work below a minimum wage is less than the total cost of welfare to all workers making less than that wage would have been in the absence of minimum wage laws.

Another consequence of price controls is lack of incentives to maintain long-lived goods such as housing. The owner of an apartment subject to rent controls has incentives to invest funds that might otherwise have been used to maintain the building in a higher-valued asset instead. Lack of "decent" housing units in rent-controlled areas of Chicago, Detroit, New York and other major cities is thus a predictable result of restrictions on private property rights.

RATIONING

To eliminate competition by personal attributes, which is an "undesirable" consequence of price controls, the government might issue coupons entitling those who get them to a specific amount of the good. Suppose you are given a coupon that entitles you to buy 20 gallons of gasoline per month at a controlled price of 30 cents per gallon. This method of resolving the allocation problem was used in the United States during World War II, in the former Soviet Union, and is being used in many parts of the world today. In fact, many U.S. legislators favored rationing of gasoline during the oil crisis in the 1970s. Rationing goes further than price controls in restricting the right of ownership. In the case of rationing, the government interferes with both transferability of ownership and exclusivity of ownership.

Let us observe two individuals whose demand for gasoline per unit of time is given in table 8-1. Data in the table are hypothetical but they conform to the law of demand, so we can use them to visualize the effects of rationing on the extent of exchange. The supply of gasoline available to those two individuals per unit of time is 60 gallons. As we know, the quantity of gasoline demanded by A and B at various prices depends on their incomes, preferences for driving, the types of cars they choose to buy, and prices of other goods (i.e., the value of that which is given up each time they buy one gallon of gas).

Table 8-1. Rationing

Price in $	Demand by A	Demand by B
1.00	30	0
.90	40	0
.80	50	10
.70	60	20
.60	70	30
.50	80	40
.40	90	50
.30	100	60
.20	110	70
.10	120	80

An implication of the difference in A's and B's demand for gasoline does not have to be that A is a richer person. My neighbor has more wealth than I do but I chose to drive more miles per day in a more expensive car, while he spends his money on monthly trips to Europe.

In the absence of governmental interference with the right of ownership and contractual freedom, the price of gasoline would tend toward 80 cents per gallon. At that price, the owner of the gasoline would get $4.80 from our two individuals. Suppose the government decides that the price is not fair to B and that price controls would give an unfair advantage to A. The government decides that each person will get a coupon entitling the bearer to 30 gallons of gasoline per unit of time at 60 cents per gallon. The gasoline owner now collects only $3.60, losing $1.20 as a result of restrictions on the right of ownership. At 60 cents per gallon, B gets all the gasoline he wants at that price, and pays $1.80 to the owner. It happens to be the same amount he would have paid for that much gasoline anyway. At the price of 60 cents, A would like to buy 70 gallons of gasoline but all she gets is 30 gallons. Those 30 gallons are worth as much as $3 to her and she gets them for only $1.80. Her gain of $1.20 is exactly equal to the owner's loss. An important consequence of rationing is a transfer of income from those who own goods to those who buy them. Moreover, rationing might redistribute income in favor of those who have a stronger preference for the rationed goods. Finally, it leaves some exchange opportunities unexploited.

Suppose the government rations gasoline but allows free exchange of coupons, as was the case in the United States during World War II. In that case, A would offer to buy some gasoline from B at a higher price. B would be happy to trade, because at a higher price he prefers less gasoline and more other things. The price of gasoline would tend to rise to 80 cents per gallon. At that price each of them would get the preferred mix of gasoline and other goods. B would have 10 gallons of gasoline which he values at 80 cents. It cost him only 20 cents. A would get 50 gallons, worth $4 to her, but would pay only $3.40.

What is the difference between rationing with and without free exchange? With contractual freedom, the extent of exchange is increased and the allocation of gasoline between competing individuals tends to be the same as in price competition. However, restrictions on private property rights change the distribution of income. In our case, the gasoline owner's loss of $1.20 is either captured by A or shared by A and B, depending on whether the market for coupons is legal. In either case, two questions must be raised. First, if the owner of a good that is rationed is not entitled to capture the full value of that good, why is someone else? Second, if the owner of a rationed good cannot capture the full value of that good, what is going to happen to that person's incentives to produce more of it?

OTHER RESTRICTIONS

If a producer could restrict potential competitors from free access to the market, that producer's profit would be enhanced. It is therefore predictable that some pressure would be brought to bear on the government to close the market to potential entrants. The reasons given for seeking such protection include encouraging innovation, protecting consumers from fly-by-night sellers, avoiding wasteful duplications, protecting workers from cheap imports, safeguarding the public interest, and others. All those reasons are at best a facade of words that serves to protect A from competition by B. Whatever the reason given for seeking protection from competition, the effect is always the same: to restrict the right of ownership. Examples are taxi services in many cities, the attitude of the American medical Association toward doctors trained abroad, liquor stores, labor unions, equal-pay-for-equal-work laws, fair employment laws, and minimum wage laws.

For example, equal pay for equal work is supposed to eliminate discrimination between various classes of employees. It surely sounds fine to take a position that one's personal taste for one class of people over another should be somehow eliminated, even though it may require a legal interference with the freedom of voluntary exchange. However, an important question is why and how the market tolerates "unequal" pay for equal work? It is difficult to imagine that profit-seeking producers are not going to bid for the services of those who are doing the same work for less. And an increase in the demand for labor services of this "discriminated against" group would then increase their rewards. To say that things do not happen that way in a private-property, free-market economy is to deny self-interest as a major motivating force.

Let us discuss the effects of legal restrictions on private property rights by going back to our VCR example. Table 7-4 is partially reprinted here as Table 8-2. The market price per VCR is \$61. C is producing 100 units at the cost of \$3,000. His total receipts are \$6,100. E is producing 200 VCRs (at the cost of \$10,000) and \$10,000 worth of other goods. Her total receipts are \$22,200.

Suppose now that E is successful in persuading the government that only she and C should be allowed to produce VCRs.

Table 8-2. Demand for VCRs

Price in $	Quantity Demanded
141	140
131	160
121	180
111	200
101	220
91	240
81	260
71	280
61	300

Being the lowest-cost producer, C gets a free ride. Whatever happens to the price of VCRs, he would continue to produce 100 units and enjoy greater revenues (and profits). Given legal protection from competition by other producers, E has incentives to search for her own best mix of VCRs and other goods. At the price of $71, she sells 180 units and produces $11,000 worth of other goods. And her total revenue increases from $22,200 to $23,780. At the price of $91, her total revenue from selling 140 units of VCRs and $13,000 worth of other things would be $25,740. Should E try to sell VCRs at $121, her total revenue would go down to $25,680. By trial and error, E would tend to choose some price between $91 and $121. Suppose it is $91 per VCR.[1] Legal protection from competition would increase E's total profits from $2,200 (at $61 per VCR) to $5,740 (at $91).

At the price of $91 per VCR (and any higher price) and the demand for 240 units, the value of the marginal unit of that good exceeds its costs of production ($50). However, the community is not going to get additional VCRs because restrictions on the right of ownership prohibit producers, whose costs of production are less than $91 per VCR from forcing E to bring the price of the marginal unit closer to the cost of producing it.

It appears that the right to be protected from competition is a property right that has money value. The value of this right is the difference between competitive (i.e. non-attenuated ownership) and protected earnings (i.e. attenuated ownership). We should expect to observe that the difference is captured by (protected) producers, lobbyists, and governments.

In general, attenuation of property rights occurs when restrictions are imposed on the uses to which a good can be put and on the freedom of the owner to transfer the rights in that good to others at mutually agreed upon price. The imposition of exogenous changes in the rules, then, affects the value of the good to the owner and to others, and affects the terms of exchange and the extent of exchange.

Henry Manne: "THE PARABLE OF THE PARKING LOTS"[2]

In a city not far away there was a large football stadium. It was used from time to time for various events, but the principal use was for football games played Saturday afternoons by the local college team. The games were tremendously popular, and people drove hundred of

---

[1] It might be in C's and E's self-interest to charge lower (than profit maximizing) prices in order to alleviate pressures to open up the market.

[2] Reprinted with permission of the author and The Public Interest, No 23, (Spring 1971), pp. 10-15. Copyright by National Affairs, Inc. 1971.

miles to watch them. Parking was done in the usual way. People who arrived early were able to park free on the streets, and latecomers had to pay to park in regular and improvised lots.

There were, at distances ranging from five to twelve blocks from the stadium, approximately twenty five commercial parking lots, all of which received some business from Saturday afternoon football games. The lots closer to the stadium naturally received more football business than those further away, and some of the very close lots actually raised their prices on Saturday afternoons. But they did not raise the price much, and most did not change prices at all. The reason was not hard to find.

For something else happened on football afternoons. A lot of people who during the week were students, lawyers, school teachers, plumbers, factory workers, and even stockbrokers went into the parking lot business. It was not a difficult thing to do. Typically, a young boy would put up a crude, homemade sign saying, "parking $3." He would direct a couple of cars into his parents' driveway, tell the driver to take the key, and collect three dollars. If the driveway was larger or there was yard space to park in, an older brother, an uncle, or the head of the household would direct the operation, sometimes asking drivers to leave their keys so that shifts could be made if necessary.

Some part-time parking operator who lived very close to the stadium charged as much as $5 to park in their driveways. But as the residences-turned-parking lots were located further from the stadium (and incidentally closer to the commercial parking lots), the price charged at game time declined. In fact, houses some distance from the stadium charged less than the adjacent commercial lots. The whole system seemed to work fairly smoothly, and though traffic just after a big game was terrible, there were no significant delays parking cars or retrieving parked cars.

But one day the owner of the chain of parking lots called a meeting of all the commercial parking lot owners in the general vicinity of the stadium. They formed an organization known as the Association of Professional Parking Lot Employers, or APPLE. And they were concerned about the Saturday parking business. One man who owned four parking lots pointed out that honest parking lot owners had heavy capital investment in their businesses, that they paid taxes, and that they employed individuals who supported families. There was no reason, he alleged, why these lots should not handle all the cars coming into the area for special events like football games. "It is unethical," he said, "to engage in cut-throat competition with irresponsible fender benders. After all, parking cars is a profession, not a business." This last remark drew loud applause.

Thus emboldened he continued, stating that commercial parking lot owners recognize their responsibility to serve the public's needs. Ethical car parkers, he said, understand their obligation not to dent fenders, to employ only trustworthy car parkers, to pay decent wages, and generally to care for their customers' cars as they would the corpus of a trust. His statement was hailed by others attending the meeting as being very statesmanlike.

Others at the meeting related various tales of horror about non-professional car parkers. One homeowner, it was said,actually allowed fifteen-year-old son to move other people's cars around. Another said that he had seen an $8,000 Cadillac parked on a dirt lawn where it would become mired in mud had it rained all day. Still another pointed out that a great deal of the problem came on the side of the stadium with the lowest-priced houses, where there were more driveways per block than on the wealthier side of the stadium. He pointed out that these poor people would rarely be able to afford to pay for damage to other people's cars or to pay insurance premiums to cover such losses. He felt that a professional group such as APPLE had a duty to protect the public from their folly in using those parking spaces.

Finally another speaker reminded the audience that these "marginal fly-by-night" parking lot operators generally parked a string of cars in their driveways so that a driver had to wait until all cars behind his had been removed before he could get his out. This, he pointed out, was quite unlike the situation in commercial lots where, during a normal business day, people had to be assured of ready access to their cars at any time. The commercial parking lots either had to hire more attendants to shift cars around, or they had to park them so that any car was always accessible. even though this meant that fewer cars could park than the total space would actually hold. "Clearly," he said, "driveway parking constitutes unfair competition."

Emotions ran high at this meeting, and every member of APPLE pledged $1 per parking space for something mysteriously called a "slush fund." It was never made clear whose slush would be bought with these funds, but several months later a resolution was adopted by the city council requiring licensing for anyone in the parking lot business.

The preamble of the new ordinance read like the speeches at the earlier meeting. It said that this measure was designed to protect the public against unscrupulous, unprofessional, and undercapitalized parking lot operators. It required, inter alia, that anyone parking cars for a fee must have a minimum capital devoted to the parking lot business of $25,000, liability insurance in an amount not less that $500,000, bonding for each car parker, and a special driving test for these parkers (which incidentally would be designed and administered by APPLE). The ordinance also required, again in the public interest, that every lot charge a single posted price for parking and that any change in the posted price must be approved in advance by the city council. Incidentally, most members were able to raise their fees by about 20 percent before the first posting.

Then a funny thing happened to drivers on their way to the stadium for the next big game. They discovered city police in unusually large numbers informing them that it was illegal to pay a non-licensed parking lot operator for the right to park a car. These policemen also reminded parents that if their children were found in violation of this ordinance, it could result in a misdemeanor charge being brought against the parents and possible juvenile court proceedings for the children. There were no driveway parking lots that day.

Back at the commercial parking lots another funny thing happened. The confusion was massive. The lot attendants could not cope with the jam-up, and some cars were actually not retrieved until next day. It was even rumored about town that some cars had been lost forever and that considerable liabilities might result for some operators. Industry spokesmen denied this, however.

Naturally, there was a lot of grumbling, but there was no agreement on what caused the difficulty. At first, everyone said there were merely some "bugs" in the new system that would have to be ironed out. But the only bug ironed out was a Volkswagen which was flattened out by a careless lot attendant in a Cadillac Eldorado.

The situation did not improve in subsequent games. The members of APPLE did not hire additional employees to park cars, and operators near the stadium were not careful to follow their previous practice of parking cars in such a way as to have them immediately accessible. Employees seemed to become more surly, and the number of dented-fenders claims mounted rapidly.

Little by little, too, cars began appearing in residential driveways again. For instance, one enterprising youth regularly went into the car washing business on football afternoons, promising that his car wash job would take at least two hours. He charged $5, and got it-even on rainy days-in fact, especially on rainy days. Another homeowner offered to take cars on consignment for three hours to sell them at prices fixed by the owner. He charged $4 for this "service", but his subterfuge was quickly squelched by the authorities. The parking situation remained "critical."

Political pressures on the city council began to mount to "do something" about the inordinate delays in parking and retrieving cars on football afternoons. The city council sent a stern note of warning to APPLE, and APPLE appointed a special study group recruited from the local university's computer science department to look into the matter. This group reported that the managerial and administrative machinery in the parking lot business was archaic. What was needed, the study group said, was less goose quills and stand-up desks and more computers and conveyers belts. It was also suggested that all members of APPLE be hooked into one computer so that cars could really be shifted to the most accessible spaces.

Spokesmen for the industry took up the cry of administrative modernization. Subtle warnings appeared in local papers suggesting that if the industry did not get its house in order, heavy-handed regulation could be anticipated. The city council asked for reports on failures to deliver cars and decreed that this would include any failure to deliver cars within five minutes demand without a new dent.

Some of the professional operators actually installed computer equipment to handle their ticketing and parking logistics problems. And some added second stories to their parking lots. Others bought up additional space, thereby raising the value of vacant lots in the area. But many simply added a few additional car parkers and hoped that the problem would go away without a substantial investment of capital.

The commercial operators also began arguing that they needed higher parking fees because of their higher operating costs. Everyone agreed that costs for operating a parking lot were certainly higher than before the licensing ordinance. So the city council granted a request for across-the-board 10 percent hike in fees. The local newspaper editorially hoped that this would ease the problem without still higher fees being necessary. In a way, it did. A lot of people stopped driving. They began using city buses, or they chartered private buses for the game. Some stayed home and watched the game on TV. A new study group on fees was appointed.

Just about several other blows fell on the parking lot business. Bus transportation in the are near the stadium was improved with a federal subsidy to the municipal bus company. And several new suburban shopping centers caused a loss of automobile traffic in the older areas of town. But most dramatic of all, the local university, under severe pressure from its students and faculty, dropped intercollegiate football altogether and converted the stadium into a park for underprivileged children.

The impact of these events on the commercial parking lots was swift. Income declined drastically. The companies that had borrowed money to finance the expansion everyone wanted earlier were hardest hit. Two declared bankruptcy, and many had to be absorbed by financially stronger companies. Layoffs among car parkers were enormous, and APPLE actually petitioned the city council to guarantee the premiums on their liability insurance policies so that people would not be afraid to park commercially. This idea was suggested to APPLE by recent Congressional legislation creating an insurance program for stock brokers.

A spokesman for APPLE made the following public statement: "New organizations or arrangements may be necessary to straighten out this problem. There has been a failure in both the structure of the industry and the regulatory scheme. New and better regulation is clearly demanded. A sound parking lot business is necessary for a healthy urban economy." The statement was hailed by the industry as being very statesmanlike, though everyone speculated about what he really meant.

Others in the industry demanded that the city bus service be curtailed during the emergency. The city council granted every rate increase the lots requested. There were no requests for rate decreases, but the weaker lots began offering prizes and other subtle or covert rebates to private bus companies who would park with them. In fact, this problem became so serious and uncontrollable that one owner of a large chain proclaimed that old-fashioned price competition for this business would be desirable. This again was hailed as statesmanlike, but everyone assumed that he really meant something else. No one proposed repeal of the licensing ordinance.

One thing happened. Under pressure from APPLE, the city council decreed that henceforth no parking would be allowed on any streets in the downtown area of town. The local merchants were extremely unhappy with this, however, and the council rescinded the ordinance at the next meeting, citing a computer error as the basis for the earlier restriction.

The ultimate resolution of the "new" parking problem is not in sight. The parking lot industry in this town is now said to be a depressed business, even a sick one. Everyone looks to the city council for a solution, but things will probably limp along as they are for quite a while, picking up with an occasional professional football game and dropping low with bad weather.

MORAL: If you risk your lot under an apple tree, you may get hit in the head.

SUGGESTED READING

Brunner, K. "The Limits of Economic Policy," in Socialism: Institutional, Philosophical and Economic Issues (S. Pejovich, ed.), Dordrecht: Kluwer Academic Publishers, 1990.

McAvoy, P. Regulated Industries and the Economy, New York: Norton, 1979.

Stigler, G. "The Extent of the Market," Journal of Law and Economics, 28, 1985.

CHAPTER 9

NON-PRIVATE PROPERTY RIGHTS, EXCHANGE, AND PRODUCTION

NON-PRIVATE PROPERTY RIGHTS IN CAPITALISM

For the most part, non-private property rights in capitalism have two organizational forms: not-for-profit firms and government bureaus.

Not-For-Profit Organizations

Not-for-profit firms are organizations whose property rights have two major characteristics. First, their assets are not transferable. Second, they have to spend the residual (i.e., the difference between their revenues and the costs of operations) to further their specific purposes. Examples of not-for-profit property organizations are private colleges, foundations, nonproprietary hospitals, fraternal organizations and churches, among others.

The absence of transferable rights in assets held by not-for-profit organizations means that no one has the right in the residual they (could) produce. An implication is that decision makers in not-for-profit firms have no incentives to seek the highest-valued uses for assets held by their organizations. What are then decision makers' incentives in not-for-profit institutions?

To address that issue we return to our football example in chapter 7. Why did we observe a shortage of tickets? Why didn't the school try to sell tickets at market clearing prices? Why didn't the superintendent or the school board fire the manager for failing to do that?

High schools are not-for-profit organizations. The manager's salary is not related to his contribution to the firm's residual. He gains little (perhaps a bit of self-esteem and a pat on the back by the superintendent) from selling tickets at market clearing prices.

Given the prevailing property rights in assets held by the firm, the manager has incentives to seek another avenue for raising his total compensation. He could try to do that by either trading favors or purchasing non pecuniary goods. For example, the manager could choose to sell tickets, and especially for the choice seats, well below their market clearing prices. By creating a shortage of choice seats, he would have something that is valuable to give. That would make the manager an important person in the community. He would be invited to parties, offered memberships in social clubs, treated to lavish meals, and so on. Or the manager could sell tickets at their market clearing prices and then proceed to spend lots of money on business trips, entertainment, a very plush office, pleasant and congenial co-workers, and other non pecuniary goods that yield satisfaction to him. Expenditures for those goods are reported as the costs of doing business.

Perhaps we can now understand why the school did not insist on selling tickets at market clearing prices. Why did Bill get the ticket? The manager may know the answer. If not, he would have failed to maximize his satisfaction.

The absence of transferable rights in assets held by not-for-profit firms (i.e., the absence of the right to capture the residual) has two general consequences. First, the performance of not-for-profit firms escapes the scrutiny of financial markets.[1] Thus, transaction costs of monitoring their managers have to be high. Second, no one has strong incentives to incur the transaction costs of monitoring expenditures by not-for-profit firms--especially, if the manager of a not-for-profit firm routinely invites members of the firm's board of

---

[1] Financial markets routinely evaluate the performance of privately owned firms via changes in the value of shares. Those evaluations represent the best judgment by those who specialize in business and finance. The effect is to raise the cost of managerial decisions that might be judged inefficient.

directors and local civic leaders to join him on various "working" trips.

State Ownership

As discussed in chapter 5, a major consequence of state ownership is that the benefits and costs of allocative decisions are dissipated throughout the economy. In comparison with the owners of resources, public decision makers have much weaker incentives to seek the best uses for state assets. Table 9-1 compares those incentives by reference to the use of a tree in private and state-owned forests. The table ignores the consequences of changes in the value of land on which the tree is planted. Data in the example are hypothetical but plausible.

Table 9-1 shows the returns from investing $100 in a live tree. From one year to another, the amount of lumber in the live tree increases. For convenience, we assume that the amount of lumber increases at a decreasing rate from the very first year. Column 2 shows the value of lumber in the live tree at the end of each year in constant prices. Like all resources, the tree has alternative uses. We can cut it and use lumber to make homes. Or we can invest the proceeds from the sale of lumber in other earning assets at the going rate of interest. It is important to understand that cutting the tree does not destroy a resource. It merely changes its use.

At the end of each year, the owner has a choice of either keeping the tree alive or cutting it, selling lumber, and reinvesting the proceeds at the going rate of interest. Driven by self-interest, the owner has incentives to keep the tree alive for as long as the rate of growth in that tree exceeds the rate of interest. For example, at the end of the third year the owner can cut the tree, sell the lumber for $304 and invest that money at the going rate of interest of, say, 15 percent. In a year, that investment would grow from $304 to $350. An alternative of not cutting the tree is clearly preferable. In one year, the value of lumber in the live tree would increase to $411. The right of ownership provides strong incentives not to cut the tree at

Table 9-1. The Value of Lumber in the Live Tree

Year	Value of Lumber	Rate of Growth
1	150	50
2	217	45
3	304	40
4	411	35
5	534	30
6	668	25
7	801	20
8	922	15
9	1.024	10
10	1,065	5

the end of third year. If the owner needed money, selling the live tree would bring at least $304. And the new owner would have incentives to let the tree grow. When the rate of growth in the value of lumber in the live tree approximates the rate of interest (year eight in our example), the owner would have incentives to cut the tree. Cutting the tree down at the end of year eight converts a valuable resource into even more valuable form of wealth.

The rate of interest is the social cost of keeping the tree standing. The rate of growth in the value of lumber is the social gain from keeping it alive. It follows that from the standpoint of the community, the best time to cut the tree in our example coincides with the owner's incentives.

When the tree is owned by the state, the decision maker in charge of running public forests may cut the tree at the end of year eight. Since the costs and benefits of cutting the tree are dissipated throughout the economy, neither that decision maker nor more senior superiors have incentives to relate the rate of growth in the value of lumber in the live tree to the going rate of interest. Hence economic analysis cannot predict whether the tree is going to be cut in that year. It really depends on the decision maker's (or superior's) private ends. And public decision makers can pursue their private ends because the costs and benefits of their choices are borne by others. There are examples of forests that have been devastated to provide governments with cash. There are also many examples in which trees were left to rot because the government was influenced by those who consider the preservation of wildlife a superior good. For example, Vice-President Al Gore in the 1990s and former Secretary of Interior James Watt in the 1980s had quite different preferences about the use of public forests.

Conservationists frequently ask for governmental controls over the use of specific resources. Their argument rests on two points: First, they assert that the actual rate of consumption of those resources is too high and should be reduced. Second, conservationists claim that many people have wrong ideas about the most valuable use for those resources. Such an argument is simply an assertion that certain people should not have their preferences satisfied.

PROPERTY RIGHTS IN SOCIALISM

The rejection of private property rights was the central premise of socialism from its earliest days. Marx and other founding fathers of socialism attributed unemployment, income inequalities, child labor, poverty, and most other social and economic problems of early capitalism to the effects of the right of ownership. Predictably, the abolishment of private property rights was the driving ideological force behind all socialist experiments in the twentieth century.

The attitude of present-day socialists has been affected by two real world experiences: (i) the failure of all socialist experiments to develop an efficient set of institutions, and (ii) theoretical research and empirical evidence about the efficiency-enhancing consequences of the right of ownership. Those two factors have created strong (survival) incentives for socialists to rewrite the doctrine in a way that would make private property rights and socialism compatible. This means that contemporary socialists must go back to drawing boards and try to to develop a new set of socialist institutions.

In the meantime, positive analysis must address the consequences of two sets of institutional arrangements that were in place long enough to be identified with socialism: the system of central planning and the labor-managed economy. The best examples of those institutional arrangements are the former Soviet Union and the former Yugoslavia. Apologists for socialism argue that by pursuing their own ends, the political leadership in the USSR and Yugoslavia ruined the chance for socialism to prove itself as a viable alternative to the free-market, private-property economy. That is a normative argument. We assume that the leaders in the Soviet Union and Yugoslavia, like all of us, pursued their own private ends within the system of incentives imbedded in socialist institutions.

The system of central economic planning and the labor-managed economy were not ad hoc models invented by and limited to a few countries. They were the consequence of the basic philosophical and economic premises of the socialist doctrine as it has evolved since the eighteenth century.

It is important to describe the basic characteristics of those two sets of institutional arrangements and analyze their effects on incentives and transaction costs. For that reason, the analysis below uses the present tense in discussing the system of central economic planning as well as the labor-managed economy.

The System of Central Economic Planning

The Ruling Elite and State Ownership. The term "state ownership" is merely a facade hiding the true owner: whoever controls the state. The major objective of the ruling elite in a socialist state is to strengthen and perpetuate its own power.[1] That is why it is important for the ruling group to control the allocation and use of resources. State ownership in resources gives the ruling elite the right to choose the allocation of resources, the right to determine the distribution of income, and the right to control entry into and exit from the power hierarchy.

The ruling elite's power to pursue its objectives is limited by its perception of the minimum bundle of rights which members of the community expect to have in return for their sacrifice of economic, civic and political freedoms. This bundle of rights is, in effect, the opportunity costs of the people.[2] The relationship between the ruling group and the people could be then treated as the *social contract*, which the people did not choose voluntarily. The power of the ruling group determines the nature of the contract, while the opportunity costs of the people define its terms (the expected minimum bundle of rights). A change in the contract would be a change in the system, while a change in the terms of the contract would reflect a change in the opportunity costs of the people. We return to this point later.

---

[1] In the former Soviet Union, the ruling elite was called the *nomenklatura*. It was about one million strong and divided into several tiers. The top tier included top party leaders, while the lowest consisted of key people in the economy, education, and scientific institutions. The nomenklatura had three sources of wealth. The salary of even a lower-tier nomenklaturist was about ten times the average salary in the USSR. The so-called approved benefits (access to special shops, special restaurants, special hospitals, special resorts, state-owned dachas,etc) were the second source of wealth. Finally, the tolerated benefits included patronage, good jobs for family members, travel abroad, tickets for entertainment events, etc. A person would earn all those benefits by being recruited into the ruling group and lose them by being kicked out of it. Thus, young people coveted an invitation to join the nomenklatura and loyalty to superiors was generously rewarded. For more details about the ruling elite in the former USSR see Voslensky, M. Nomenklatura. New York: Doubleday, 1984.

[2] The following goods figured most prominently during pre-Gorbachev years: guarantee of employment, undemanding work pace, slow but steady rise in living standard, and stable prices.

The Mechanism of Economic Planning. Economic planning means that vertical relations (administrative orders) replace horizontal relations (contracts). Administrative orders flow from the top leadership through various bureaucratic channels down to productive units. The economic plan is in effect the sum total of those orders. Given the ruling's group preference for the allocation of resources, the distribution of income, and the output mix, the central planning agency and its subordinate units--whose major function is to provide economic and technical solutions for decisions and directives issued by the ruling group--begin the job of preparing the annual economic plan. In terms of standard economic theory, the planning bureaucracy has to find a way to keep the economy on the production frontier (the efficiency requirement) and to produce a mix of outputs corresponding to the point on the production frontier chosen by the ruling group (the allocation requirement).

The planning bureaucracy usually begins its preparation of the economic plan by sending preliminary production targets, via its hierarchy, to the industries and firms. Those preliminary production targets are based on the past performance of enterprises, new capacities, new priorities, hoped-for changes in productivity, and other indicators. Enterprises, which are at the bottom of the planning hierarchy, are answerable only to their bureaucratic superiors, who monitor their compliance with the plan, evaluate the attainment of production priorities, and administer rewards and punishments.

Given their production targets, enterprises must be able to count on an adequate supply of inputs. However, to allow firms to purchase supplies in open markets could easily modify the plan's objectives and frustrate the will of the ruling elite. Thus, economic planning must include the planning of supplies. In the former Soviet Union, the bureaucracy controlled the allocation of about 40,000 inputs, and production plans of about 500,000 firms of one kind or another. The allocation of inputs to enterprises, the so-called supply plan, then, is an essential part of the system of central economic planning. *Material balances* play a key role in preparation of the supply plan. They are drawn for all products in physical units.[1] The balance for each input shows its sources (e.g, inventory, current production, imports) and uses (e.g., inventory, current production, exports). On the basis of material balances and production targets, the allocation of inputs to individual enterprises is negotiated between relevant ministries or other state agencies. Several layers of bureaucracy are involved in the process of making, monitoring and enforcing the supply plan.

The problem is that even a small deviation from the supply plan causes a chain reaction throughout the system. Suppose the firms producing screws and bolts fail to deliver them on time to other firms. The latter's rate of output would be immediately affected. Next, enterprises that depend on those firms' outputs would be affected. And so on. Suppose the planners allocate additional coal, steel and labor to the firms producing screws and bolts. To do this they have to reduce the allocation of coal, steel and labor to other firms. And they must reduce the planned rate of output of these firms, as well as of other firms that depend on them, and so on. To make adjustments and revisions of the plan possible, the ruling group must design low- and high-priority areas and use administrative orders to shift resources from the former into the latter. In the former USSR low-priority areas were agriculture, services and consumer goods.

The manager of a firm in the system of central economic planning is required to submit to superiors detailed information about the firm. And the manager gets back marching orders. The economic plan leaves little room for discretionary decisions by enterprises, for those decisions could be in conflict with the ruling group's objectives.[2] Vertical contracts (i.e., the economic plan) determine which factory is going to make bicycles, how many, to whom they are to be delivered, and at what prices. That is, in transmitting the firm's

---

[1] Material balances could be drawn in monetary terms if prices of individual inputs were administratively controlled.

[2] Given the penalty-reward system for managers and lower level bureaucrats (see chapter 13) and the high transaction costs of monitoring their behaviors, the ruling elite has incentives to keep the Pandora's box closed.

plan from the top to the bottom of the planning hierarchy, the firm's superiors are exercising their administrative authority over the firm rather than responding to the flow of information and initiatives by the manager.[1]

The flow of information up the bureaucratic ladder and the flow of orders down to the bottom of the bureaucratic hierarchy is the essence of economic planning. Goods are not bought and sold in a planned economy. They are delivered.

Transaction Costs in a Centrally planned Economy. The absence of market signals in a planned economy makes the transaction costs of deciding who should do what, preparing the plan, and checking the reports by subordinate units for accuracy higher than in a private property economy.[2] Subordinate units in the system of economic planning have strong incentives to maintain and enhance the transaction costs of monitoring their performance.

Transaction costs specific to the system of central economic planning are the value of human and nonhuman resources needed to (i) enforce the plan;[3] (ii) prepare the economic plan;[4] (iii) maintain and protect the rules of the game;[5] and (iv) prevent managers of business firms and lower administrative agencies from falsifying their reports to superiors.

---

[1] Of course, if the leaders wanted to make allocation of resources based on individual preferences they wouldn't need to plan anything.

[2] A major audit in 1981 found that about one third of audited reports in the Soviet Union contained some distortions.

[3] By suppressing the process of bidding for goods, the ruling elite deprives the economy of a low-cost method of determining the value of resources in alternative uses.

[4] Preparations involves assignment of production targets, allocation of supplies, and supervision of the execution of the plan.

[5] Compare the size of armed forces, the role of security forces, the number of political prisoners in planned and free-market countries.

Given the staggering cost of information about the available supplies of resources, alternative production techniques, and the capabilities of the existing firms, economic planners need a stable relationship between monetary and real magnitudes. For that reason, most prices and the minimum supply of money needed for carrying out real transactions specified in the plan have been subject to strict administrative controls in the former USSR. Business firms were not allowed to keep cash balances (those could support nonplanned transactions) and they had to make all payments to other firms and agencies by transferring budgeted balances from one account to another. The ruling elite was simply excersizing its right of ownership. In comparison, state-owned firms in capitalist economies are also subject to numerous restrictions and are given their budgets, but *they purchase supplies in the market.*

Spontaneous Development of Informal Channels of Influence. While the common objective of the top leaders in centrally planned economies is to preserve and enhance the prevailing institutional structure, members of the leadership have strong incentives to seek ways to enhance their own positions within the group. Those incentives include being alert to internal alliances within the "summit," and appointments (and promotions) of friends to important posts in the ruling elite. The consequences of those incentives were quite similar in all centrally planned economies and are worth noting because of their historical as well as analytical value.

Pursuing incentives based on the marriage of political power and economic wealth (a major consequence of state ownership), members of the top leadership created their personal "courts." Then, pursuing the same set of incentives, members of the court gathered around each top leader formed their own courts, and so on. In this manner, informal channels of influence developed in centrally planned economies. Predictably, those courts were in competition with each other for power and influence. An implication of the existence of such competing channels of influence in socialist states was that their bureaucracies became less concerned about the substance of policies handed down by the bureaucratic hierarchy, and more interested in discovering who made them and who was pushing them. Reaction to policies was then affected by the balance of power between competing courts. Ministries, industries and enterprises sought changes in their administrative orders through their own or a friendly court. Informal channels also created a market for "insiders" who traded on information about issues debated at the higher levels of government. Jan Kowalski, a Polish economist, notes: "Some top politburo member can give an order without feeling constrained by laws....Whether his orders will be actually executed remains questionable."[1] This informal political structure explains the "purges" in the former USSR. Whenever a member of the top leadership died or "retired" from power, members of all that leader's court were quickly retired, too. Unlike other Soviet leaders, Stalin frequently changed the composition of the politburo. Thus, he had to purge a larger number of people than his successors.[2] Recently, a top Soviet spy explained the working of those courts in gruesome details.[3]

Attempts to Save Socialism: The Case of Perestroika in the Former USSR. The purpose of perestroika in the late 1980s was to save the Soviet system by adjusting the terms of the social contract to changes in the opportunity costs of the people. These had changed in the 1980s for a number of reasons, including loss of faith in the inevitability of socialism (i.e., the present value of the costs of

---

[1] Kowalski, J. "Rational Expectations in Centrally Planned Economies," in (S. Pejovich, ed.) Socialism: Institutional, Philosophical and Economic Issues, Dordrecht: Kluwer Academic Publishers, 1987, p.187.

[2] Similar informal channels of influence and appointments to friendly "courts" are observed in the public sector of a private property economy (patronage, political appointments, etc.). In the private sector, it is costly for the owner to discriminate by personal characteristics--hiring a less productive friend could bankrupt the firm.

[3] Sudoplatov P. and Sudoplatov, A. Special Tasks, Boston: Little Brown and Company, 1994, especially pp. 292-317.

"building" socialism increased relative to people's perceptions of the present value of promised benefits); loss of faith in the ability of the ruling elite to fulfill the terms of the implicit social contract with the people; and the rise of a pragmatic, educated and consumption-hungry younger generation.

Perestroika addressed three critical problems of the system of central economic planning: how to make firms more efficient, how to reduce shortages, and how to curb the power of the bureaucracy. We review them in turn.

In a centrally planned economy, the ruling elite allocates capital goods to business firms, transfers existing capital goods from one enterprise to another, and decides what to do with investment funds. The firm cannot sell, rent, or modify capital goods in its possession. It can only use them to produce (and overproduce) its prescribed output target. Since the firm pays no rent for the use of capital goods, the manager considers capital goods to be a free reserve. There is no penalty for having too much capital (relative to the firm's output target), and the excess capital comes in handy for breakdowns and emergencies. The manager of a centrally planned firm has incentives to press administrative superiors for more capital. By making the Soviet manager's rewards depend on the firm's profitability (defined as the ratio of profits to the stock of capital), the ruling elite was hoping to influence managerial behavior through turning accumulated reserves of capital into a liability. However, to make the Soviet manager cost-oriented and interested in minimizing holdings of capital, the prevailing property rights in capital goods had to change. The ruling elite had to give the manager the right to control not only the firm's replacement capital but also new additions to the firm's stock of capital; that is, the mix of output produced by capital goods industries. But to grant the manager this right, the ruling elite had to give up its own right of controlling output produced by capital goods industries. The choice was to leave the Soviet manager frustrated in pursuing the new incentives.

Perestroika proposed to deal with the shortage of supplies by allowing business enterprises to negotiate contracts with each other. Free contracting for supplies meant that voluntary horizontal relations among enterprises would replace vertical administrative orders. To make this reform operational, the ruling elite had to transfer two property rights from itself to the firm. First, because the output of one firm is the supply of inputs for another, the Soviet manager had to have the right to decide who to produce for and by implication how much to produce. Second, the implementation of free contracting requires competitive markets and scarcity prices (so that managers could know the opportunity costs of the inputs used by their firms). The ruling elite never got around to transferring those property rights to business enterprises.

Predictably, perestroika had few friends in the Soviet ruling elite, especially among the middle and lower echelon members. From their standpoint, the only relevant costs of perestroika were those borne by themselves. And the relevant cost of any specific institutional change had to be the effect of that change on the power and privileges of a cluster of nomenklaturists. Given the principal-agent costs of monitoring the nomenklatura, and uncertainty about the opportunity costs of the people, Gorbachev had to make some difficult choices. He had to assume either that the opportunity costs of the people had risen in excess of the cost of perestroika to the nomenklatura, or that the costs borne by the nomenklatura were still greater than the benefits people expect to get from perestroika. It appears that Gorbachev couldn't decide which way to go and shifted his position on several occasions until he was, in effect, overthrown by both.

A Comparison of central economic planning and free market competition. Let us illustrate how property rights affect incentives in a free-market economy and in a centrally planned economy by looking at two fundamental issues: who gets what (the allocation issue) and who does what (the production issue).

Suppose that people in Denver decide, for whatever reason, to eat more beef. As the demand for beef per unit of time increases, a grocery store in Denver discovers that its inventories of meat are being depleted. Driven by desire for more wealth (they keep what they make less taxes), the owners call the slaughterhouse in Chicago to increase their weekly orders of beef. The slaughterhouse owners in turn discover that their inventories of beef are being depleted. So they call a rancher deep in the heart of Texas to increase the weekly shipment of cattle. However, the rancher might not be able to satisfy their increased demand for cattle immediately. Even in Texas it takes time to breed larger herds. Whether the rancher informs the slaughterhouse that the price of cattle is higher, or the slaughterhouse offers to pay more for additional cattle, or the grocery store in Denver "bribes" the slaughterhouse to supply more beef, the price of beef is going to be bid up. People whose demand for beef has not changed are then going to buy less beef at a higher price. And the amount of beef they release is the amount of additional beef that people whose demand for beef has increased are going to get.[1] An increase in the price of beef, then, is necessary to decide who gets how much from the given supply of beef. At a higher price for beef, less efficient ranchers have incentives to start raising cattle (remember the production of VCRs in Table 7-3). An increase in the price of beef thus performs another critical function: deciding who should produce additional supplies.

Suppose now that the same situation occurs in a centrally planned economy like the former USSR. As the demand for beef per unit of time increases in, say, Kiev, a grocery store discovers that its inventory (or the length of the line of customers waiting in front of the store) of beef is being depleted. The manager is legally responsible for passing that information to an administrative superior,[2] who is likewise legally responsible for informing another administrative superior. Information about a change in the demand for beef in Kiev travels up the planning hierarchy. While in a private property economy information about a change in the demand for any good has the force of a command, the central planning agency may respond to

---

[1] Here we recall the law of demand; as the price of beef goes up, people in Denver would still demand more beef but not as much more as they demanded at the old price.

[2] The manager has neither the power nor incentives to ask for additional beef.

a change in the demand for any good if and only if an adjustment in the allocation of resources would not interfere with the objectives of the plan (i.e. the ruling elite). Not having the choice of satisfying their desire for more beef by raising their offer (and having beef transferred to them from those whose demand has not changed), people in Kiev must either get to the meat store first, or find a way to trade favors with the store manager. Price controls or not, the price of beef in Kiev would go up in a way that is arbitrary and associated with high transaction costs.

The Labor-Managed Economy

In 1948, the Yugoslav economic system was a carbon copy of the Soviet-type economy. After it was thrown out of the Soviet bloc in 1948,[1] the Yugoslav ruling elite embarked on a series of institutional changes. The purposes of these changes were several: to maintain the political and economic monopoly of the ruling elite, to preserve state ownership rights in most resources, to open the economy to trade with the West, and to improve the production efficiency of the system. By the mid-1960s, the Yugoslav system of labor participation in the management of enterprises had captured worldwide attention.

Disappointed with the performance of the Soviet-type economy, critics of the right of ownership saw the labor-managed economy as a long-hoped for alternative to capitalism. By paying no attention to the fact that its institutions did not emerge spontaneously, the supporters of the labor-managed economy ignored incentives and transaction costs specific to the system.

The turning point in Yugoslavia's departure from the system of central economic planning was the 1950 passage of the Law on Management of Enterprises by Workers' Collectives. The 1951 Law on the Management of Capital Goods by Enterprises clarified the

---

[1] There are many theories why Stalin threw Tito out of the socialist bloc. For our purpose here, the only thing that matters is that the two leaders parted their ways in 1948.

issue of handling the firm's assets, by giving workers' councils a sui generis property right over the firm's nonhuman assets: the right of use. The firm was allowed to sell its assets to other firms and to change the composition of its assets. However, the firm also had to maintain the value of its assets via depreciation allowances and reinvestment of the proceeds from sale of capital goods. The Law of Banks of 1961 started a long, and perhaps the most difficult, process in the development of the labor-managed economy: the search for a method of allocating investment funds in an environment in which the ruling group has the right of ownership in capital goods, while the working collective has the right to appropriate the flow of returns from those assets. The labor-managed economy of Yugoslavia continued to evolve throughout the 1960s and early 1970s. The method of its evolution was the same: exogenous legal changes consistent with private ends of Marshall Tito and his associates.

In process, the labor-managed economy in former Yugoslavia became and still is the only labor-managed economy that has ever been tried on such a large scale. Its major institutional features were: (i) state ownership of capital goods, (ii) the employees' ownership of the returns from capital goods, (iii) the employees' right to govern the firm, (iv) the substitution of bank credit for the system of administrative distribution of investable funds, and (v) the system of quasi-contracts between all economic agents. The labor-managed firm with its incentives and transaction costs is discussed in some detail in chapter 13.

SUGGESTED READING

Ioffe, O. and Maggs, P. The Soviet Economic System: A Legal Analysis, Boulder: Westview press, 1987.

Pejovich, S. "A Property Rights Analysis of Perestroika," Communist Economies, 2, 1990.

Pejovich, S. "A Property Rights Analysis of the Yugoslav Miracle," Annals of the American Academy of Political Science, 1990.

Voslensky, M. Nomenklatura, Garden City: Doubleday, 1984.

Chapter 10

INSTITUTIONS AND ECONOMIC DEVELOPMENT

All societies have to allocate resources between present and future consumption, evaluate investment alternatives, provide an orderly flow of consumer goods between production dates (e.g., wheat between harvests), and encourage the growth of wealth.

INTEREST RATES AND EXPECTATIONS

In a private property economy those goods that provide future services are valued in financial markets. The market price of such goods is the present value of their expected future services discounted at the prevailing rate of interest.[1] Since nonowned goods are not transferable, there is no way to price their expected future benefits. Predictably, financial markets do not exist in state-owned economies.

In financial markets people purchase four types of assets: (i) claims to future amounts of money (bond markets), (ii) claims to capital good (stock markets),(iii) claims to future consumer goods (futures markets), and (iv) claims to land and buildings (real estate markets). Since our expectations about future events are continuously revised and interpreted differently by different people, there is constant buying and selling of claims in financial markets. The right of ownership provides for the transferability of those claims. And contractual freedom, via the bidding process across financial markets, pushes toward an equality the rate of return on capital goods, the rate of interest on bonds, and the community's valuation of future consumption relative to current consumption.

---

[1] I invest $1 and get back $1.20 one year later. The net productivity of my investment is 20 percent. If the going rate of interest was 10 percent and the return of 20 percent was anticipated by some people, my asset would quickly have been revalued to about $1.10.

The rate of interest is the money price of earlier rather than later availability of nonmoney goods. Just as the price of A places a value on the bundle of other goods that must be forgone, interest rate is the rate of exchange between one unit of A now and a bundle of A tomorrow. Earlier availability of goods offers a greater range of choices than later availability (sometimes called preference for current over future consumption), and also offers an opportunity to use goods now to produce more goods tomorrow (growth of wealth). Thus, the rate of interest is positive in all societies.

A change in interest rate means a change in the present value of capital goods relative to their costs of production. For example, suppose an asset costing $1,000 has a life expectancy of ten years and promises the residual (after all costs) of $142 per year. The net productivity of this investment is about 7 percent. At 6 percent interest, the present market value of this project would be $1,045. At 8 percent interest, the value of the project would be $952. The rate of interest is a means for comparing the value of expected services from capital goods to their current costs of production. It is plain wrong to think of the rate of interest as being only the rate at which we lend and borrow funds. The interest rate is much more than a cost of investment.

Anticipation of future events also affects present prices of assets. Suppose a firm announces a new product. If enough members of the community happen to be optimistic about the product, the price of a share of the firm's common stock will increase to reflect those expectations. Suppose, however, that a firm is located in a country where a political party advocating restrictions on private property rights is gaining public support. Expectation about the firm's future profits will be revised downward and the price per share will drop.

The right of ownership and contractual freedom are essential if the capitalization process is to function. Restrictions on the right of ownership and/or contractual freedom raise transaction costs of establishing the prices that correctly reflect current expectations about future events. The absence of property rights makes the comparison between the future value consequences of alternative current decisions all but impossible.

THE GROWTH OF WEALTH

The idea of economic development has dominated both the aspirations and the public policy of most countries since the end of World War II. Yet, only a few countries have been able to accomplish anything in this area. For example, at the time of independence East Asia and Africa faced similar economic conditions of life but chose different development paths. Many countries in East Asia encouraged the right of ownership and foreign investments, while most African countries chose state ownership and discouraged private investments from abroad. Today, East Asia is a model of economic success, while Africa suffers rising poverty and hunger.[1] Moreover, in the United States, the median income of Asian-Americans, whose behavior is marked with a strong work ethic and accumulation of private wealth, exceeds the median income of white Americans.[2]

Most developing countries attribute their low rate of growth of wealth to a variety of causes, including an inadequate resource base, shortage of capital, exploitation by their former colonial rulers, and poor development planning.

The exploitation argument is increasingly becoming an embarrassing one to offer as an excuse for economic stagnation. After several decades of being sovereign nations, most developing countries appear to be in much worse economic shape than they were in the years following their independence.

Lack of resources is another standard explanation for low rates of economic growth in the third world. However, economic evidence

---

[1] In an interesting article, Keith Richburg discussed the issue of why African development has lagged so far behind that of East Asia, which suffered from a similar set of obstacles. See Richburg, K. "Why is Black Africa Overwhelmed While East Asia Overcomes?" International Herald Tribune, July 14, 1992, pp. 1,6.

[2] Median household income for Asian Americans was $36,784 and for whites was $31,435. See "Two Measures of Household Income," New York Times, July 24, 1992, p. 10.

does not support the contention that the availability of resources ensures a high rate of economic growth. Much depends on what people do with resources they happen to have. If an inadequate resource base is responsible for poverty in India, why is a resource-poor country like Japan doing well? If overpopulation is a problem in China, why are people in Hong Kong and Singapore so much better off? Russia and the Ukraine are certainly resource-rich in comparison with Holland and Belgium. For centuries the Texas plains were among the most uninviting areas of the world but within a century the area has become one of the most affluent regions on earth.

It is also difficult to accept the argument that a shortage of capital is holding back economic development in Eastern Europe, Africa, Central and South America, and many parts of Asia. Private capital is a very mobile resource that is highly responsive to higher yield opportunities. The flow of capital to low growth regions has been kept back by political instabilities, currency controls, restrictions on the right of ownership (especially repatriation of profits), noncredible legal institutions, discriminatory taxes, and corrupt governments. Compare the flow of capital to Japan and India, East Asia and Africa, and the Czech republic and Romania.

At one time economists in many third world countries (and in the West) believed that competent leaders and good planning could assure high rates of growth. This belief was indirectly supported by "published" rates of growth in the former USSR in the 1950s and 1960s. Empirical evidence suggests that the growth of wealth has been higher in those countries that have done more to protect the right of ownership and contractual freedom than in other countries, regardless of their respective availability of resources, rates of savings, and population growth. An implication is that a cause-effect relationship exists between alternative property rights and the flow of innovation. That is the issue to which we now turn.

PROPERTY RIGHTS AND INNOVATION

Innovation could be the development of a new good, the opening up of a new market, a new source of supply, a new method of production, or a new method for reducing transaction costs. Whichever the case, by injecting a novelty into the flow of economic life, the innovator offers the community a *new* choice. The voluntary acceptance or rejection of the innovation reveals the community's evaluation of the costs and benefits of the novelty. Acceptance moves resources to higher-valued uses, while the rejection leaves the community in the same position. An implication is that one set of institutions may be superior to another set not because it happens to be technically more efficient in terms of the standard maximization paradigm, but because it encourages the flow of innovation with concomitant expansion of the opportunity set. Innovation is, in effect, a trade-off between the allocative efficiency within the prevailing opportunity set and an increase in the opportunity set. Voluntary acceptance of innovations by the community means that a reduction in the former is compensated by an expansion in the latter.

Innovation explicates the meaning of economic development into the expansion of choices.

Innovation cannot be planned. Business firms and governments cannot decide to have three innovations per month. Innovation is triggered by the individual in the pursuit of economic gains. The individual must perceive an opportunity to do something new, have incentives to face the risk of introducing the novelty into the system, and have the power to carry out the innovation. The innovation is implemented through the firm[1] or contracts across markets. In either case, the pursuit of economic gains through innovation depends on the prevailing rules of the game. The issue of economic development then boils down to the effects of alternative institutions on the flow of innovation. We can break down the issue of how to enable individuals to attempt to innovate into: freedom to

---

[1] This could be either the firm for which the innovator works for or one formed by that innovator.

innovate, incentives to innovate, the power to innovate, and evaluation of innovation.

Freedom to Innovate

Since innovators do not come from a specific social class, the larger the number of people who have the freedom to innovate, the higher is the probability of increasing the flow of innovation, all other things being the same. Three important factors determine the pool of people who are free to innovate: the right to choose the method of organizing production, the right to acquire resources, and the right to use them. In a private property economy, everyone has the right to acquire resources and use them to pursue any lawful activity, including innovation. The owners of resources (or their hired managers) can choose from a variety of organizational structures ranging from small proprietorships to large corporations, and from cooperatives to not-for-profit firms. A private property economy places no restrictions on individuals' freedom to innovate.

However, restrictions on the right of ownership frequently interfere with the owner's right of exclusive use of an asset or its transferability. Codetermination laws in Germany prescribe a definite method for organizing production in large firms.[1] License requirements for entry into many occupations are quite common in Western Europe. The regulation of pharmaceutical products in the United States offers an example of the consequences of restrictions on the right to use one's assets. Karl Brunner commented:

> The tragically crippled and deformed babies resulting from the use of thalidomide by pregnant women influences....regulatory policies. The measures implemented raised the costs of development for new products by a large factor...Innovation declined by a sharp margin and the appearance of new drugs sharply contracted...A policy

---

[1] See chapter 12.

addressed to minimize the probability of bad products maximized at the same time the probability of NOT having useful drugs.[1]

It would be wrong to argue that regulatory policies have no benefits. The point is that they impose some heavy costs. Restrictions on the method of organizing production raise the cost of equity capital in financial markets. License requirements reduce the number of people who have the right to acquire resources. Protectionism and monopoly privileges limit one's right to use resources. In general, the attenuation of private property rights restricts the freedom to innovate.

In a centrally planned economy, entry into decision making is through membership in the ruling elite, which is a self-perpetuating group joined primarily through personal connections, and from which one departs through death or political disgrace. The ruling elite, as a group, controls both the formation of new enterprises and the allocation and use of resources. Individuals (including members of the ruling elite) have no right to acquire productive resources.[2] A remarkable 1957 book by Vladimir Dudincev[3] has not aged with the passage of time. It describes the frustration of trying to innovate in an environment in which the potential innovator does not have the right to acquire and use resources. Members of the ruling elite, managers of enterprises, and all other individuals who perceive an opportunity for an innovation must sell the idea to their colleagues or superiors, who in turn have to sell it to their superiors, and so on. The right to

---

[1] K. Brunner, "The Limits of Economic Policy," in (Pejovich, S. ed.) Socialism: Institutional, Philosophical and Economic Issues, Dordrecht: Kluwer Academic Publishers, 1987, pp 41-2.

[2] Categorizations such as a private property, a centrally planned, or a labor-managed economy define only the dominant property right in that country, but there are always others. Thus, there was a small private sector in the former USSR and some innovating activity surely occurred in that sector.

[3] V. Dudincev, Not By bread Alone, New York: E.P. Dutton & Company, 1957.

acquire and use resources in a centrally planned economy is then effectively limited to the ruling elite.

In a labor-managed economy, the pool of those who have the right to acquire and use resources is restricted to the working collective. The term "working collective" is important here. Individual employees can neither acquire productive assets nor determine their uses. Only the working collective as a whole can do so either directly by referendum or through its own governing board, which is usually called the workers' council. An employee who perceives an opportunity to innovate must sell the ideas to the workers' council, a group of people with limited business experience, diverse attitudes toward risk, inadequate understanding of production techniques and market processes, and short time horizons.

Incentives to Innovate

Innovation introduces a novelty into the system. A successful innovation yields benefits in excess of what the bundle of resources used by the innovator was earning before. However, in that an innovation is a nonroutine activity, the risk associated with it is not known. The innovator has in effect to make a choice between investing a bundle of resources in the innovation the outcome of which is unpredictable, or in one of the routine activities for which the risk is known. The latter is the cost of innovation. The innovator's decision must depend on that individual's incentives to accept the uncertainty associated with the outcome of the innovation.

In a private property economy, the innovator can appropriate the present value of the expected benefits from a successful innovation either in one lump sum (by selling it to another person) or as a stream of payments. However, large profits attract duplications and imitations from existing as well as potential rivals. Thus, the present value of the benefits from a successful innovation depends on how long the benefits are expected to last. In discussing incentives to innovate, it is important to recognize that contractual freedom provides incentives to innovate even for those who do not own the resources. For example, the manager of a firm benefits from initiating an innovation through the market for managers, where the current profitability of the enterprise operated by that manager determines his future income.

A successful technological innovation provides the innovator with a temporary monopoly position, primarily by creating a gap between the new technology and average technology. This technology gap is both an intrafirm and an interfirm phenomenon. A former chairman of Texas Instruments asserted that Texas Instruments' most successful technological innovations are at least ten times more productive than the company's average technology.[1] In fact, if all firms were able to adopt technological innovations quickly, incentives to develop new technologies and new products would be seriously impaired. The gap between the best and average practice, which is the source of the innovator's gains, endures because it is costly for firms to learn and evaluate new technology. Some firms also make wrong bets about the best practice (e.g., Montgomery Ward after World War II). As we saw in chapter 6, transaction costs might slow down the firm's rate of adoption of new technology. In general, imitation of a successful innovation requires expenditures of resources and time. And the innovator's choice between routine investments and innovation depends on the expected length of the imitation lag.

The prevailing property rights in a labor-managed economy (i.e., the absence of transferable claims on the returns from capital goods) have two consequences that tend to dampen the collective's incentives to innovate. First, the absence of the right to capitalize the expected future benefits into their present market price means that the working collective cannot appropriate the expected benefits of a successful innovation in one lump sum. Second, since the collective can capture the benefits only as they occur, its members (e.g., those who expect to retire soon or change jobs) must have a bias against innovations that are expected, if successful, to yield benefits over a long period of time.

---

[1] Haggerty, P. "The Corporation and the Individual." Dallas: University of Dallas Press, 1979, p.13.

On the surface, the manager and all other individuals in a centrally planned economy are free to *propose* an innovation to their superiors in the ruling elite. However, there is a world of difference between the right to make suggestions and the right to do things. For at least two reasons, a member of the ruling elite has reduced incentives to try to push an innovation through the channels. First, decisions to innovate in the system are not individual decisions. They are reviewed and debated by layers of various committees. Thus, they are time-consuming and could rock the boat. Second, an individual who believes in a specific innovation finds the private costs of pushing it through the channels substantial. If the innovation is a success, the innovator will share the benefits with colleagues and superiors. If it is a failure, colleagues and superior will blame the innovator.

The Power to Innovate

Freedom to acquire and use resources is not the same thing as having actually the power to get them. In a private property economy, capital markets match the quantity of financial assets demanded with the quantity supplied to reflect contractual agreements on various issues, including risks. The ability to acquire an asset in financial markets depends on the borrower having enough resources to pay for it, and the lender having a bundle of rights in the asset and being willing to transfer these at a price the borrower is willing to pay.

The ability of a privately-owned firm to innovate is more likely to be limited by transaction costs arising from its organizational structure and size than by financial markets. The larger the firm and the greater the number of people who have to say "yes" as an innovation unfolds, the more costly it is to carry out the innovation. Moreover, a major issue facing the management of successful firms in a private property economy is how to preserve flexibility, creativity, and adaptability as the company gets bigger and its initial vigor yields to the process of maturing. Pat Haggerty, a founder of Texas Instruments, remarked that the firm's top management spent many months trying to find a way to institutionalize the process of proposing, approving and implementing innovations so that the company could retain its leadership in technology. Given those issues, it appears that private property rights provide an institutional framework within which new firms (e.g. computer firms in recent years) can innovate, while mature firms have an opportunity for rebirth.

In a labor-managed economy, the nontransferability of the employees' claims on the firm's cash flows and the fact that those nontransferable claims are also contingent on people's employment with that firm reduce the collective's ability to innovate. The absence of financial markets leaves the labor-managed firm with two major sources of investable funds: retained earnings and bank credit. The former is not a likely source of funds for innovation. A loss of retained earnings is borne by the entire collective now, while the gains have to be shared with new employees. The ability of the labor-managed firm to innovate, then, depends on the banking system.

The ability to innovate in a centrally planned economy is limited to those innovations that are approved by economic planners.

Evaluation of Innovation

A novelty does not necessarily make people better off. It has to be voluntarily accepted and integrated into the economy. In a private property economy, competitive markets evaluate the novelty. Freedom of exchange reveals the costs and benefits of the novelty as perceived by interacting individuals. And those costs and benefits, via relative prices, tell us whether or not the innovation has enriched the social opportunity set.

The critical role of the individual in a free-market economy lies not in "sovereignty" (i.e., guiding the choice of outputs) but in evaluating innovations proposed by entrepreneurs and in influencing future activities in the economy by accepting or refusing those innovations.

R. Nelson and S. Winter have identified two vehicles by which a successful innovation is integrated into the system: competition and the quest for knowledge.[1] The competition thesis is as follows. In a private-property economy, profits attract attention. New firms then enter the industry and join the old ones in competing with the innovating firm. The flow of resources from lower- to higher-valued uses continues until monopoly profits are eaten up via lower prices to consumers and higher prices to resource owners. This type of atomistic competition dominates the integration of innovation into the economy where the firms are relatively small or the source of innovation lies outside the industry.

The quest for knowledge argument applies to a successful innovation in new technology that could, at least temporarily, be shielded from competing firms. The mechanism for integration of innovation into the economy comes through successive investments into research and development by rival firms (e.g., the Model T, Polaroid).

Integration of innovation in a labor-managed economy has three limitations. First, a successful innovation creates larger profits for the collective. The absence of financial markets raises the cost of information to potential rivals. Second, as information about larger profits becomes available, only existing firms enter into competition with the innovating firm. The entry of new firms in a labor-managed economy has to be slow because it requires a group decision. Third, suppose that rival firms have to hire additional workers in order to compete with the innovating firm. Given the prevailing property rights, new workers are new policy makers as well. This means that the current collective has incentives to trade off some pecuniary income that could be had by hiring additional workers for the security of its common interests.

In a centrally planned economy, the absence of both private property rights and contractual freedom (i.e., competitive prices)

---

[1] Nelson, R. and Winter, S. An Evolutionary Theory of Economic Change, Cambridge: Harvard University press, 1982.

makes the costs of knowing whether the community has or has not accepted an innovation staggeringly high.

SUGGESTED READING

Moore, J. "Measuring Soviet Economic Growth: Old Problems and New Complications," Journal of Institutional and Theoretical Economics, 148, 1992.

Nelson, R. and Winter, S. An Evolutionary Theory of Economic Change, Cambridge: Harvard University Press, 1982.

Posner, R. Economic Analysis of Law, Boston: Little, Brown and Co, 1992, chapter 15.

Schroeder, G. "The Implementation and Interpretation of Innovation in Soviet-Type Economies," Cato Journal, 9, 1989.

PART THREE

THE FIRM

Chapter 11

THE FIRM AND CONTRACTS

METHODS OF ORGANIZING PRODUCTION

Basically, the process of production can be organized in two ways. You might enter into a contractual agreement with one person to grow wheat on your land, with another to harvest it, with a third to store it, and with a fourth to sell it. This method of organizing production is called contracting across markets. You negotiate a separate agreement with contractual partners and pay each of them an agreed-upon sum of money (or whatever else you agree to give them) in exchange for a specific performance.[1]

The costs of contracting across markets include identifying the lowest-cost partners, negotiating contracts, renegotiating contracts in response to changing circumstances,[2] and reducing the probability of opportunistic behavior. An advantage of contracting across markets is that the cost of shirking is borne by the shirker, who is paid the same amount of money (less possible damages) whether fulfilling that side of the bargain in five hours or five days.

Alternatively, you might hire those four people to work for you. In that case, you are the central contractual agent in a team production process. Contractual agreements are still present, but they are different. You pay your employees a specific sum of money (wages) in exchange for the right to tell them what to do, when to do it, and how to do it. This method of organizing production is called

[1] As we saw in chapter 9, economic planning is a form of nonvoluntary contracting.

[2] Reopening of the Suez Canal after the 1956 war between Egypt and Israel led to numerous renegotiations (and suits) of contracts to build oil tankers, most of them having to do with the size of tankers.

the firm. The firm is not a one-person enterprise; it is a group of people in teamwork.

The team method of production is costly, too. Employees are paid a contractual wage per period of time, which means that the cost of shirking (reduced output of the firm) is not borne by the shirking worker. Clearly, employees have incentives to shirk, and the firm must then incur the cost of monitoring them. Next, the team method of production requires specialists to supervise the division of tasks up and down the chain of production. Finally, the firm has to meter the performance of individual inputs because its output is an inseparable bundle produced by many cooperating inputs. There is no way to tell who has contributed how much to the total product. Yet, the firm's survival in competitive markets depends on how successful it is in establishing a positive relationship between the rewards and productivity of cooperating inputs.

Business firms exists because teamwork is an efficient method for organizing production. Some twenty years ago Armen Alchian wrote:

> The wealth growth of General Electric derives precisely from the superiority of its internal markets for exchange and reallocation of resources--a superiority arising from the greater (cheaper) information about people and proposals. Many knowledge effects that would be externalistic in an ordinary market are converted into beneficial internalities within the firm as incentives and rewards to those producing them.[1]

Limitations on the supply of managerial skills, transaction costs, and the complexities of large operations eventually increase the cost of the team method of production relative to the cost of contracting across markets. Those firms that are successful in discovering less costly mix of internal transactions and outside contracts have a better chance of

---

[1] Alchian, A. "Corporate Management and Property Rights," in The Economics of Property Rights (E. Furubotn and S. Pejovich, eds.), Cambridge: Ballinger, 1974, p. 142.

survival in competitive markets. And transaction costs differ from one industry to another and even from one product to another. For example, the cost of supervising one hundred waiters in a restaurant is likely to exceed the cost of controlling one hundred workers on the assembly line in a manufacturing plant.

Conventional wisdom is that the firm is a black box that has its own objectives. However, business firms, governments and other organizations have no objectives. Only individuals do. That is why changes in the leadership of business firms, governments, and other organizations matter. To understand the behavior of any organization, economic analysis has to identify the individuals who make decisions for that organization, the rules (primarily property rights) under which they make decisions, their incentives, and the transaction costs of monitoring their performance. Instead of asking, "Why does IBM (or the U.S. government or Texas A&M University) behave as it does?" it is more appropriate to ask, "Why does the decision maker in this organization behave in a certain way?" Only individuals have objectives; only individuals can make decisions; the behavior of individuals depends on the incentive structures and transaction costs; and the prevailing property rights influence both the incentive structures and transaction costs.

Treating the firm as a black box that exists in order to satisfy the relevant marginal conditions teaches little. Members of the team have conflicting objectives. The performance (survival) of the firm depends on cooperation and coordination among members of the team. And cooperation and coordination among team members depends on contractual agreements they have with each other. The function of those agreements is to resolve the conflicting objectives of the team members. Some types of contracts pass the market test and are imitated by others. While the terms of those contracts might differ in specific details from one firm to another, they attach specific names to different types of firms, such as corporations, partnerships, cooperatives, labor-managed firms, etc. Rather than being a black box, the firm serves as a nexus for a set of contractual relationships among individuals.

Neoclassical theory of the firm has three shortcomings. First, it describes the tendencies only in the restricted case of the private property firm with zero or low transaction costs. Second, neoclassical theory treats the firm as a black box. Finally, it views the gains in productivity as arising from specialization among independent producers rather than from successful internal contracting among the team members.

CONTRACTS AND REWARDS

In a very interesting example, Armen Alchian and William Allen discuss the effects of several types of contractual agreements on the performance of teamwork.[1]

There is an island called Fishland. On this island 1,000 people fish for a living. They fish from the shore and each of them averages four fish per day. The total daily catch is thus 4,000 fish. Then a boat is found. The boat makes it possible for some to fish on the ocean. Table 11-1 provides hypothetical data on the various quantities of fish that can be caught by varying the number of people on the boat.[2] Neoclassical economics would say that five people would end up fishing from the boat and that the community would have 4,014 fish. However, we observe teams that continue to produce "inefficient" outcomes. This does not necessarily mean that some people are less competent than others or ignorant. It means that incentives and transaction costs matter. The Fishland example in Table 11-1 looks into the effects of several types of contractual agreements among the team members on the total output.

---

[1] Discussion in this section is adapted from Alchian, A. and Allen, W., Exchange and Production, Belmont: Wadsworth Publishing Co 1983, chapter 8.

[2] Net social marginal product in column five is the marginal product on board less the opportunity costs of four fish from the shore.

Share and Share Alike

Suppose that those already on the boat share daily catch and also to control jointly how many, if any, additional persons are to be invited to fish from the boat. Under this type of agreement, members of the team have incentives to use the effect of an additional person on their own average daily catch as the criterion for determining whether that person should be allowed on board. In our case, the number of people on the boat is likely to be three. The total output of 4,012 fish then falls short of the social maximum of 4,014. The entire gain of 12 fish is captured by people allowed to fish from the boat. Labor-managed firms and some professional associations such as doctors, lawyers, musicians and electricians are examples of this type of teamwork.

If and when such payments were legal and not too costly to collect, those already on board would have incentives to invite additional people to fish from the boat at a price of a daily entry fee. Clearly, the fee must assure the newcomer of a little more than four fish per day, and, at the same time, make those on board a little better off. In our example, taking a fourth person on the boat would reduce the average daily catch from 8 to 7.5 fish. However, the fourth person could pay a fee of 3 fish per day and keep 4.5 fish for himself. Those already on board should be happy to accept a fee-paying newcomer because they would end up with 8.5 fish per day. This type of arrangement is found in many country clubs and some labor unions.

Table 11-1. Fishland

Number of Men on Board	Total Catch on board	Marg. Product on board	Average Product on board	Net Social MP	Social Total
0	0	0	0	0	4,000
1	6	6	6	2	4,002
2	16	10	8	6	4,008
3	24	8	8	4	4,0012
4	30	6	7.5	2	4,0014
5	34	4	6.8	0	4,0014
6	36	2	6	-2	4,0012
7	36	0	5.14	-4	4,008
8	32	-4	4	-8	4,000
9	27	-5	3	-9	3,991
10	21	-6	2.1	-10	3,981

Source: Alchian, A. and Allen, W. Exchange and Production, Belmont: Wadswort Publishing Company, 1983, p. 164.

In every case, the risk of fluctuations in the daily catch (bad luck, fish not biting, bad weather, problems with the boat, etc.) is borne by members of the team. The only way for them to avoid this risk is to quit the boat. The cost of leaving the boat is the difference between the average daily catch from fishing on the ocean and the expected daily catch from the shore, for people on board receive the flow of benefits only for as long as they are members of the team. Also, each member of the team has incentives to shirk. A shirking worker captures all the benefits of that action and shifts the costs of reduced output to the team. For example, one person sleeps for a few hours (without co-workers noticing this absence) and the total catch of fish is reduced from 24 to 21. They all get seven fish. The shirker has traded one fish for several hours of leisure. That is a voluntary choice and we have to assume that the shirker is better off. The other two people lost one fish each. The following quote describes a situation comparable to that of a labor-managed firm:

> On the Yangtze River in China, there is a section of fast water over which boats are pulled upstream by a team of coolies prodded by an overseer using a whip. On one such passage an American lady, horrified by the sight of the overseer whipping the men as they strained at their harness, demanded that something be done about the brutality. She was quickly informed by the captain that nothing could be done: "Those men own the right to draw boats over this stretch of water and they have hired the overseer and given him his duties."[1]

The story makes an important point. The extent of shirking under this kind of contractual arrangements depends on both transaction costs of monitoring members of the team as well as the monitor's incentives to punish (e.g., fire) nonperformers. The last point is quite important. The monitor in a labor-managed firm, being appointed and fired by members of the team, has incentives to please them.

The Discoverer of The Boat Has The Right of Ownership

Suppose the man who found the boat and became its owner hires people, pays them wages to fish for him, and keeps everything (i.e., the residual) that is left after all contractual obligations are met. To hire someone, the owner must pay that person just a little over four fish per day. He has incentives to hire five people. The marginal

---

[1] McManus, J. "The Cost of Alternative Economic Organizations," Canadian Journal of Economics, 8, 1975, p. 335

product of hiring the fifth equals that person's opportunity costs. The total output of 1,014 fish is equal to the social maximum. The owner captures the entire gain of 14 fish per day. Moreover, he can sell the boat for a lump sum of money equal to the present value of the expected future catch during the life of that boat. As Alchian and Allen note:

> The coincidence between maximum private and maximum social gain is not accidental. People with private property rights who seek profits is an open market system will maximize the social total...it is not a contrived quirk of our special example, and it happens without the profit seeker's intent or a central directive authority.[1]

The owner has incentives to monitor members of the team. Moreover, he has incentives to seek innovations that would reduce transaction costs (i.e., economize on the use of resources) of monitoring his employees. The owner can avoid the risk of fluctuations in the catch (i.e., changes in his wealth) by selling the boat and capturing the value of expected future gains in one lump sum. This is true of all privately owned resources. In the private property economy, each individual can select the type and amount of risk. Some people buy oil wells (or sell them to avoid unforseen changes in wealth) while others take on rental properties, some invest in junk bonds while others prefer Treasury Notes, etc. An important implication of private property rights is that resources are transferred from less optimistic to more optimistic individuals.

Contracts to Rent

Instead of hiring people to work for him, the owner might rent the boat to a person or a group of people. The question is then how many people are likely to end up on the boat, and what is the maximum

---

[1] Alchian, A. and Allen, W., Exchange and Production, p. 167.

rent the owner can extract from them? If the owner rented his boat to three people, their total catch would be 24 fish, or 12 fish over and above their opportunity costs. The maximum rent the owner can get with three people renting the boat is thus a bit below 12 fish. If the owner rented the boat to five persons, their total catch would be 34 fish, or 14 fish over and above their opportunity costs. Given the data in our example, the maximum rent the owner can get is then just about 14 fish. The outcome seems to be the same as in the previous example (hiring people at a wage of 4+ fish).

What then is the difference, if any, between the owner hiring five people and renting the boat to five people? Assuming perfect foresight about the daily catch, there is no difference. But in a world of uncertainty and imperfect knowledge,[1] the two arrangements are not the same in terms of incentives and risk. Under the hiring arrangement, the owner bears the costs (and gets the benefits) from unforseen fluctuations in the daily catch. Under the leasing arrangement, the renters bear those costs in the short-run. Also, they have no incentives to maintain the boat properly. Michael Jensen and William Meckling conclude:

> The obvious agency costs of the rental arrangement are those associated with the reduced incentives for the user to maintain the asset properly, to guard it from theft, and the increased incentives to misuse it...The magnitude of these costs along with monitoring and bonding costs that would be incurred in the effort to control them explains why rental of most durable goods is not observed. It is simply a more costly contracting arrangement.[2]

---

[1] As indicated, the daily catch may fluctuate for a number of reasons such as bad weather, fish not biting, bad luck, negligence and shirking.

[2] Jensen, M. and Meckling, W. "Rights and Production Functions," Journal of Business, 52, 1979, p. 480. They define agency costs as the sum of the monitoring expenditures by the principal, the bonding expenditures by the agent, and the residual loss.

Everyone Can Fish From The Boat

Suppose that the government decides that the boat is communal property (belongs to the "people"). In that case, everyone who wants to fish from the boat can do that. How many people would end up on the boat? As long as the average product on board exceeds four fish, people will have incentives to continue joining the crew. Eventually, there will be eight people on the boat, each of them catching just about as many fish as they could catch from the shore. The community ends up with 4,000 fish. No member of the community is better off. And no one has incentives to maintain the boat.

Government Decides Who Can Fish From The Boat

Suppose the government appoints a manager who is told to maximize income from the right to fish on the ocean. The profit of 14 fish goes to the state. It would appear that the only difference between private and state ownership is who gets the profit. However, that is not true. In a world of uncertainty and incomplete knowledge, the maximum profit is not known in advance. The issue is what are decision makers' incentives to discover and seek larger profits, and what are the transaction costs of monitoring their behavior? The owner of a resource has incentives to maximize profits and to incur the costs of monitoring employees. On the other hand, no one in the government can appropriate the residual, incentives to invest time and effort to seek the best profits are certainly not very strong, and no one bears the entire risk of making inefficient decisions. The loss is shared by taxpayers. The actual outcome thus depends on the private ends of those who manage government-owned resources, private ends of their superiors, and the superiors' transaction costs of monitoring managers. This is not to say that decision makers in government will never try to maximize profit. But compared to the private owner, they simply have weaker incentives to do so.

Limitations of The Fishland Example

It does not discuss the effects of different contractual agreements on transaction costs.[1] Second, while showing, quite correctly, that private property rights in the boat create incentives to maximize the social output, the example also implies that the boat owner is the only beneficiary of the growth in output. That is not so. Under the regime of private property rights, people would have incentives to own more boats. And the cost of making new boats (in terms of fish forgone) would control the rate at which new boats are produced. In the process, market competition would transfer income from the owners of boats to those who own the resources required to make boats (via higher prices for those resources) and consumers (through lower price of fish). Finally, the market competition continuously creates new knowledge (better fishing areas), stimulates innovations (better technology), and encourages imitations of successful activities.

TEAMWORK, CONTRACTS, AND TRANSACTION COSTS

Firms exist because they are the organizations for teamwork. Teamwork is a set of contracts involving separately owned (or controlled) resources whose value as a team exceeds the sum of the market values each could earn separately. The source of the gains is those contracts. They are the agreements about (i) future performance of members of the team, and (ii) metering performance and rewards. The critical importance of metering productivity and rewards arises from the fact that the firm's output is produced by many cooperating inputs, and there is no way to tell who has contributed how much to the total product.

By resolving the conflict of interests among members of the team, successful contracts enhance their coordination and cooperation.

---

[1] Laszlo Szakadat, a perceptive economist from the University of Budapest, made some useful observations about Fishland during a seminar in Bratislava in March 1994.

And the commitment to work together reduces transaction costs. Unlike the firm in neoclassical theory which assumes that the marginal productivity of inputs determines both the total output and its allocation, the contention here is that in a world of uncertainty and incomplete information, different kinds of contracts (constrained by prevailing property rights) create their own incentives and transaction costs. Those incentives and transaction costs then, through their effect on rewards, encourage productivity responses. Jensen and Meckling wrote:

> Statutory laws set bounds on the kinds of contracts into which individuals and organizations may enter without risking criminal prosecution....Thecourts adjudicate conflicts between contracting parties and establish precedents which form the body of common law. All of these government activities affect both the kinds of contracts and the extent to which contracting is relied upon. This in turn determines the usefulness, productivity, profitability and viability of [business firms].[1]

The sources of transaction costs in business firms are *bounded rationality* and *opportunism*. In one way or another, bounded rationality has been discussed throughout this book. It simply means that in a world of uncertainty and incomplete knowledge, individuals have different subjective perceptions of the real world and limited ability to predict the future. As noted in the Fishland example, an important implication of bounded rationality is the allocation of risk under different property rights. Here, we add only a few additional points.

A major difference between capitalism and socialism involves their respective effects on the distribution of risk. In a private property economy, the individual can sell a risky asset and invest proceeds in private savings. You can take money from the bank and

---

[1] Jensen, M. and Meckling, W., "Theory of the Firm: Managerial Behavior, Agency Costs and Ownership Structure," Journal of Financial Economics, 3, 1976, p. 311

invest in a risky venture. An individual can keep an oil well, hoping that its reserves are large, or sell it and invest proceeds in less risky assets. I can be paid my opportunity cost and bear the risk of changes in the demand for my skill. Or I can shift that risk to my employer (at a price) through a long-term employment contract. In a socialist-type economy, no individual can avoid bearing risk. The nontransferability of assets provides no room for specialization of risk bearing across individuals with different degrees of risk aversion.

In a private property economy the risk of changes in the value of resources is borne by those who own them. For example, I purchase a share of Texas Instruments for $100. In effect I tell the firm: "You are better experts at making money than I am. Please take my $100 and do the best you can for me." That is, I choose to become a member of the TI team because my subjective perception is that it is the best I can do for myself. I can always take the market value of my investment back.

In a socialist economy I can neither choose risk nor avoiding bearing it. One can vote with one's feet, but that is a costly alternative. Implications for transaction costs in capitalism and socialism are obvious. In a socialist economy, those who bear risk and those who are in a position to economize on transaction costs are not the same people. That is, incentives to resolve contractually the conflicting objectives of individuals with respect to risk are much weaker and not always possible. In a capitalist economy those incentives are strong.

Opportunism follows from bounded rationality and self-interest. Armen Alchian and Susan Woodward defined opportunism and its implications for transaction costs as follows:

> When a conflict arises between what people want and what they have agreed to do for others, they will act in their own interest insofar as it is costly for others to know their behavior (others face costly information)....Opportunism covers more than the propensity for mutually reliant parties to mislead, distort, disguise, obfuscate, or otherwise confuse in order to expropriate wealth from one another. It includes honest

> disagreements. Even when both parties recognize the genuine goodwill of the other, different but honest perceptions can lead to disputes that are costly to resolve.[1]

The so-called Lange-Mises controversy is a good example of failure to recognize the importance of transaction costs arising from opportunism. Oscar Lange and Ludvig Mises conducted a major debate on the proposition advanced by Lange that the planned economy could duplicate the results of the private property economy if the managers of socialist firms were instructed to maximize profits. Neoclassical theory provided the framework for the debate. Given its assumption of zero transaction costs, managers of socialist firms had to follow instructions. Hence the debate focused on the comparison of equilibrium solutions. The result was an impeccable technical discussion that wasted lots of resources on wrong questions. Recognizing that positive transaction costs encourage opportunistic behavior, relevant questions should have been: What is the socialist manager's survival trait? What is the penalty-reward system under which that manager operates? What is the cost of monitoring the manager's behavior? What would the manager gain from pursuing planned objectives? Could the manager do better by pursuing another kind of activity?[2]

Opportunism has two basic forms: *hold-up* and *moral hazard*. Both create incentives to prevent opportunistic behavior via reductions in transaction costs. However, those incentives have different consequences. Hold-up explains incentives for vertical integration, while moral hazard explains the principal-agent conflict.

To understand the implications of hold-up it is necessary to distinguish between specific and general resources. A resource is specific to the firm if the wealth of the owner of that resource is affected by the behavior of other members of the team. Usually, large

---

[1] Alchian, A. and Woodward, S., "The Firm is Dead; Long Live the Firm," Journal of Economic Literature, 26, 1988, p. 66.

[2] The final two chapters of this book address those questions.

sunk costs create opportunities for hold-up. For example, I own the only elevator in a building. The building is specific to my elevator. That is, I can affect the building owner's wealth by restricting the use of elevator to certain hours or claiming frequent repairs. The building owner would then either have to reduce monthly rental or lose tenants. By holding him up, I could appropriate (by raising rental for the elevator) the difference between daily revenues from the building and daily operating costs plus the daily equivalent of the building's salvage value; or the difference between daily revenues from the building and the daily equivalent of the cost of another elevator; or the difference between the total revenue per unit of time and the value of the specific resource to the second highest valuing user (per unit of time).[1] Frequently, resources are specific to each other (e.g., oil well, pipeline and refinery). Resources are general if the wealth of their owners does not depend on the behavior of any specific member of the team (e.g., tenants in the building paying market price for office space, or the owner of furniture used in the building's lobby).

Those who own resources specific to the firm have incentives to protect themselves from opportunistic behavior by other members of the team.[2] The prevailing property rights specify those incentives and, at the same time, define constraints on contractual agreements which carry them out. In a private property economy, owners of firm-specific resources have incentives to protect themselves against hold-up via vertical integration or long-term contracts. The latter could be either explicit legal contracts or market-enforced arrangements. Vertical integration, i.e. joint ownership (i.e., elevators and buildings, oil wells and pipelines) virtually rules out opportunistic behavior but might run into problems with government agencies such as Federal Trade Commission, Federal Communication Commission, the Antitrust

---

[1] For excellent analysis and numerous examples see Klein, B., Crawford, R. and Alchian, A., "Vertical Integration, Appropriable Rents, and the Competitive Contracting Process," Journal of law and Economics, 21, 1978.

[2] Include bureaucrats in charge of controlling the use of resources owned by the government.

Division of the Department of Justice, and public sentiment against "monopolies." Long-term contracts do not eliminate opportunistic behavior but might be efficient (i.e., bypassing legal problems with the government) when the appropriable rent is low or contracts are relatively inexpensive to specify and monitor (goodwill, brand names, rental of land). At any rate, protecting firm-specific assets from opportunistic behavior reduces transaction costs. And lower transaction costs translate into higher productivity for the firm.

Moral hazard (or postcontractual opportunism) occurs when one party to a contract relies on the behavior of another party and information about that behavior is costly. The source of moral hazard is agency costs and plasticity of resources. Jensen and Meckling explained agency costs as follows:

> If both parties to the relationship are utility maximizers there is good reason to believe that the agent will not always act in the best interests of the principal....it is generally impossible for the principal or the agent at zero cost to ensure that the agent will make optimal decisions from the principal's viewpoint. In most agency relationships the principal and the agent will incur positive monitoring costs....we define agency costs as the sum of: (i) the monitoring expenditures by the principal, (2) the bonding expenditures by the agent, (3) the residual loss.[1]

Resources are plastic when the agent has a wide range of discretionary legitimate choices and the principal faces high transaction costs of ensuring that a particular agenda is pursued. For example, teachers have a great deal of freedom from their academic superiors to teach what they like. Researchers in drug companies could easily spend their time experimenting with new drugs rather than improving known and profitable ones. Imagine the shareholders' and/or debt holders' controlling fashion designers. In contrast,

---

[1] Jensen, M. and Meckling, W., Theory of the Firm, Managerial behavior, Agency Costs and Ownership Structure," Journal of Financial Economics, 3, 1976, p.308.

railroads, steel-producing firms, pizza establishments and utilities are not plastic. Because of high costs of preventing opportunistic behavior (not because of higher risk), firms with plastic assets should be expected to find borrowing more costly. A testable implication is that firms with plastic assets have relatively lower debt-equity ratios. Alchian and Woodward made the following point:

> By"plastic" we do not simply mean risky. Oil that has only to be pumped and sold is highly implastic. The optimal rate at which to pump the oil depends on the pattern of prices over time, and there is little in the way of possibilities for exploiting an oil well either by increasing the riskiness of its value or by changing its product into personal consumption. But an oil is a risky asset.[1]

CONCLUSION

Teamwork is an efficient method for organizing production because the value produced by the team exceeds the sum total of the value that cooperating inputs could produce outside the team. We observe business firms because they are organizations that involve teamwork. The dependency of some team members on other members means that the efficiency (that is, a positive residual) of the firm depends on the nature of contractual agreements among team members. Contracts are supposed to resolve the conflict of interests among team members and enhance their cooperation and coordination, especially including the agreement on metering productivity and rewards. Prevailing property rights constrain the scope and extent of contractual agreements. An implication is that economic analysis of the firm must internalize the contracting and the property rights system within which the firm operates. Moreover, economic analysis of exchange and production

---

[1] Alchian, A. and Woodward, S., "The Firm is Dead; Long Live the Firm," Journal of Economic Literature, 26, 1988, p.69.

must *internalize* the process of development of and changes in institutions.

Some types of contractual agreements pass the market test and are imitated by other teams. From one firm to another those contracts differ in details and especially in informal codes of communications, but they eventually come to be identified with types of firms, such as producers' cooperatives, codetermining firms, mutual associations, corporations, and partnerships. The types of firms we continuously observe in the real world must have survived in competition with other types of firms (e.g., corporations) or secured a legal protection from competition (e.g., codetermining firms). The former class of firm has obviously discovered an efficient set of contracts. Equally obviously, the latter class of firms has not.

The next two chapters discuss four different types of firms. Two of those, corporations and codetermining firms are observed in private-property, free-market economies and two, government-owned and labor-managed firms, are more common in a socialist society.

SUGGESTED READINGS

Alchian, A. and Woodward, S. "The Firm is Dead: Long Live the Firm," Journal of Economic Literature, 26, 1988

Jensen, M. and Meckling, W. "Theory of the Firm: Managerial Behavior, Agency Costs and Ownership Structure," Journal of Financial Economics, 3, 1976

Klein, R., Crawford, R and Alchian, A. "Vertical Integration, Appropriable Rents, and Competitive Contracting Process," Journal of Law and Economics, 21, 1978

Chapter 12

CAPITALIST FIRMS

What does it mean when we say that a firm is privately owned? For example, suppose Judy wants to have a Bible shop. She rents a building, borrows money from a local bank to buy equipment, and hires several people to work for her. Laura, on the other hand, wants to run a pornography shop. She owns the building, uses her savings to buy equipment, and members of her family volunteer to help her in the shop. It could appear that Laura owns her business, while Judy has a long way to go to become the owner of the Bible shop. In fact, they both own their respective businesses. Why? Because the ownership of the firm is about *rights.* To say that a firm is privately owned means that the owner has a bundle of rights in that firm. Three important rights that define the privately owned firm are:

1. The owner's right to the revenue of the firm. The revenue is used to pay all members of the team their contractual prices. Any residual belongs to the owner. The owner's right to appropriate the residual indicates two sets of incentives. First, the owner of the firm has incentives to own firm-specific assets (or the individual who owns firm-specific resources has incentives to pay for the right to control the team). Because the ownership of the firm provides an efficient protection against opportunistic behavior by the owners of nonspecific resources. *The privately owned firm is then a set of contracts between the owners of cooperating inputs with one party who is common to all the contracts.* Second, the owner's right to appropriate the residual creates incentives for the owner to monitor the performance of team members, to reduce shirking in the firm, to enhance cooperation and coordination of team members, to meter performance and reward employees in accordance with their efforts and productivity, and to

change the mix of contracts across markets and team production in response to successful innovations in technology and managerial practices.

2. The owner's right to hire and fire members of the team. Absence of the right to choose members of the team would weaken the owner's power to search for a larger residual. This second right presupposes the freedom of contract. The owner is free to fire employees or sue them for damages arising from a breach of contract. Employees have the same right. They can "fire" the employer by quitting or sue for damages from a breach of contract. The owner is then the central contracting agent rather than a disciplinary authority; an owner has no power to discipline or punish employees, only the right to choose the team. Therein lies the problem with various legal and administrative rules that weaken the owner's right to withdraw from a contract with a team member (i.e., to fire an employee). By restricting freedom of contract, those rules in effect raise the cost of production. That is, as the threat of firing is reduced, the owner's ability to monitor the performance of team members is impaired.

3. The right to sell the two rights specifies above. The most essential characteristic of ownership is capitalization of the expected future consequences of current decisions into present values. The right to transfer one's rights to others at a mutually agreed-upon price is a basic component of the right of ownership. And the market price of a firm is the present value of the expected residual over the firm's life discounted at a rate of interest and adjusted for expected changes in the owner's right to fire and hire members of the team. In a world of uncertainty and incomplete information, individuals have different subjective perceptions about the future. Some are more optimistic than others. Transferability of ownership then implies a transfer from less to more optimistic individuals. To call it a transfer from less to more productive people would imply perfect foresight.

Two critical consequences of the right of ownership on the behavior of the firm are then: (i) the owner's right to

capitalize the expected future consequences of current decisions about the use of the team into their market prices, and (ii) the owner's right to bear changes in the value of the firm.

The former eliminates the owner's time horizon because the flow of benefits over the productive life of the firm is available to the owner in one lump sum. The latter creates strong incentives for the owner to seek an ever larger residual.

The analysis of the firm is then both simple and straightforward. First, we recognize that in a world of uncertainty and incomplete information, the subjective perceptions individuals form about their opportunity sets and trade-offs must differ from one person to another. Second, we identify the bundle of property rights in business firms under various institutional arrangements. Next, we determine the resultant incentive structures and their effects on the kinds of contractual agreements that emerge through innovations and imitations. Finally, we deduce the implied behavior of the firm and examine the analytical propositions yielded by analysis against empirical observations.

Compared to neoclassical analysis of the firm, the property rights approach, then, provides a framework for an admittedly less formal but more predictive analysis of the behavior of a wider class of business enterprises both within a given set of institutions and under different institutional arrangements. We literally do not know if any firm has ever maximized its profit or operated on its efficiency frontier. Economic analysis cannot answer that question. But it can tell us how and why private property rights and free contracting create incentives and lower transaction costs of moving resources to their higher-valued uses.

We now examine two different kinds of business firms in capitalism, one that emerged voluntarily, and one that was imposed by fiat.

THE MODERN CORPORATION

In a private-property, free-market economy, those who own labor, capital and other resources are free to negotiate with each other any kind of teamwork agreement they want. Some types of contracts pass the market test and are repeatedly observed. From one firm to another, those contracts differ in details and especially informal codes of communication (i.e., internal "cultures"), but they attach specific names to different types of firms such as producers' cooperatives, labor cooperatives, codetermining firms, mutual associations, not-for-profit firms, partnerships, corporations, and others. All those types of firms exist in the United States (and Western Europe). They have all been organized voluntarily and survived competition from other types of business organizations. No law in the United States dictates the terms of contractual relations among the team members. Yet, the corporate firm has, spontaneously, become the dominant contractual form. What are advantages of the corporate firm over other types of private-ownership enterprises?

Technological development around the time of the industrial revolution, improvements in transportation, and the emergence of large political entities in place of feudal princedoms made mass production of goods possible, relatively inexpensive, and profitable. However, mass production of goods required large start-up investment in fixed assets subject to hold-ups. That is, business firms, needed a large amount of capital to exploit technological advances and marketing opportunities.

The rule of unlimited liability made the application of new techniques difficult to finance. With each partner held personally liable for the entire debts of the firm, it was too difficult for existing partners to accept new ones. Every partner could impoverish others through incompetence or opportunistic behavior. Moreover, the rule of unlimited liability made absentee ownership costly. In short, the rule restricted equity financing.

In response to economic pressures from within the system, numerous contractual agreements were tried to resolve the problem of pulling together large amounts of capital. Eventually a new legal concept evolved: the rule of limited liability.[1] This law limited each owner's liability to the market value of that individual's investment in the firm. Equity investments were divided into small shares, which were traded in financial markets. The breaking up of equity interests into relatively small shares made it possible for corporate firms to attract funds from small savers.

It follows that the corporate firm has all the advantages of private ownership firms plus more. The corporation has proved to be the most effective method of *voluntarily* gathering large amounts of capital for long-lived ventures. This advantage derives from the anonymous alienability of shares. Anonymity is made possible by limited liability. Individual owners of the firm (shareholders) need not care who other owners are. This enables shareholders to buy and sell shares without requiring the approval of other owners of the firm. That translates into a substantial reduction in the transaction costs of raising large amounts of capital.

The owners of the corporation are entitled to capture the residual, to hire and fire cooperating inputs, and to sell those rights in financial markets. Other members of the team are holders of fixed claims. The shareholders have the right to choose contractual partners as well as incentives to monitor their performance.

However, the ownership of many corporations is dispersed among many shareholders. This means that individual owners face high transaction costs in monitoring managerial decisions. Thus, their right to hire and fire the firm's management is attenuated. Critics of the private property economy have seen the attenuation of the right of ownership as creating fundamental conflicts of interest between the shareholders who bear risk and the managers who manage risk.

---

[1] Perhaps the best source on the corporation and the rule of limited liability is Easterbrook, F. and Fischel, D. The Economic Structure of Corporate Law, Cambridge: Harvard University Press, 1991, especially chapters 1-2. For a different analysis of the rule of limited liability see Tollison, R. "The Voluntary Origins of the Corporate Contract," Scholl Foundation Lecture Series, Texas A&M University, 1982; and Ekelund, R. and Tollison, R. Mercantilism as a Rent-Seeking Society, College Station: Texas A&M University Press, 1981.

First, they claim that by divorcing ownership from control, the dispersion of stockholding "trivializes" the meaning of private ownership in corporations. It is interesting to note how hard-core socialist scholars from Eastern Europe, such as Branko Horvat from Croatia and Mihailo Markovich from Yugoslavia, have shifted their criticism of private property rights. Some decades ago, people like them blamed private ownership for transforming humanity into a horde of profit-seeking beasts. Today, they argue that there is no need to encourage the development of private-ownership firms because the dispersion of shareholding has already "socialized" private property rights. The argument is simply wrong. As discussed in Chapter 11, when I buy a share of General Electric, I voluntarily transfer my "control" rights to those who, in my judgment, are much better at making money. I choose to who I give my money. And I can always choose to take the market value of my investment back.

Second, critics of the corporate firm assert that by raising the owners' costs of monitoring corporate managers, dispersion of stockholding leads to an inefficient transfer of wealth from shareholders to managers.[1] If that were so, we should expect to observe a reduced flow of resources into the corporate sector because of lower rates of return on investment.

Empirical observations are consistent with neither of these two criticisms. How do we explain the fact that millions of individuals continue to invest in common stock? Why do they not choose other forms of investment? Why is equity financing not being driven out by investments in fixed claims? Why do we not observe a lower bid price for stocks of corporations with dispersed ownership? Why do dispersed ownership corporations not have lower rates of growth of shareholders' wealth?

---

[1] The claim is something like this: positive transaction costs enable managers to substitute away from the firm's profit to gain various nonpecuniary sources of satisfaction for themselves. Since one dollar in cash is worth more than one dollar in nonpecuniary income, the transfer of wealth from shareholders to managers is inefficient. Moreover, a consequence of understating the profit is a lower than socially desirable flow of resources into the corporate sector of the economy.

In fact, extensive empirical and theoretical research has demonstrated that the dispersion of shareholding does not have the inefficiency effects expected by corporate critics because competitive markets guard the shareholders' wealth. Central to this research are the effects of private property rights on transaction costs via (i) financial markets, where market valuation of the expected future consequences of current decisions by managers raises their costs of making decisions that are contrary to the interests of shareholders, (ii) the competitive markets for managers, and (iii) quite importantly, hostile takeovers, leveraged buyouts, and going-private decisions. According to Michael Jensen, these market-oriented methods of disciplining corporate managers have made increased operating efficiency of corporations, employee productivity, and shareholder value.[1]

In conclusion, the modern corporation has all the advantages of a private-ownership firm plus the ability to raise large amounts of capital for long-lived investments. The owners' bundle of property rights creates strong incentives for management to seek higher-valued uses for resources.[2] And competitive markets reduce the shareholders' costs of monitoring corporate managers.

---

[1] See Jensen, M. "Eclipse of the Public Corporation," Harvard Business review, September-October 1989, and Jensen, M. and Ruback, R. "The Market for Corporate Control," Journal of Financial Economics, 11, 1983.

[2] The objective of the team does not have to be ever larger residual: the contracts may call for other objectives as well (i.e., Wall Street Journal, New York Times).

The Separation of Ownership from Control: A Case Study[1]

The separation of ownership from control is frequently taken to reflect a major weakness of the corporate firm. The separation thesis is understood to imply a loss of effective control by stockholders over managerial decisions that affect the value of their wealth. The underlying cause of this separation of ownership from control is the dispersion of stockholding. Combined with management advantages in a proxy fight, the dispersion of stockholding increases the shareholders' costs of hiring, monitoring and firing their managers. Given their subjective estimate of transaction costs, corporate managers can substitute away from potential profits to pursue their own private ends. Those policies, in turn, suggest a reduction in the efficiency of the corporate firm.[2] Yet, there is no evidence that the dispersion of stockholding has reduced incentives for resources to seek their higher-valued uses. Why?

An observable implication of the separation thesis should be a negative relationship between the dispersion of stockholding and the owners' gains in wealth; that is, a lower bid price for stocks of corporation with dispersed ownership. A meaningful test of this presumed implications of the separation thesis must start with the circumstances that affect the agency costs. An important circumstance is the relationship between current managerial decisions and their evaluations in financial markets. This linkage between current managerial decisions and changes in stock prices reduces the owners' transaction costs of detecting and evaluating the performance of their managers. To test the separation thesis we asked the following question: Do dispersed corporations have lower rates of growth of stockholders wealth than less dispersed firms?

---

[1] Based on Koshal, R. and Pejovich, S. "A Note on the Separation of Ownership from Control," Management International Review,32, 1992. Illustrations, tables and detailed statistical results are not reprinted here.

[2] When transaction costs are positive and the manager raises his total income by on-the-job consumption, the reported profits fall short of the firm's potential profits. The flow of resources is then stops short of the efficient allocation of resources.

For lack of better data, we used the percentage of the firm's stock held by institutions as a proxy for dispersion assuming that institutions are more likely to incur the cost of detecting and policing managerial decisions. Thus, an increase in the percentage of the firm's stock held by institutions is taken to imply a reduction in the dispersion of ownership.

We defined the rate of growth of stockholders' wealth as follows:

$$R_t = \frac{E_t + P_t - P_{t-1}}{P_{t-1}}$$

where E = annual dividend per share, P = stock price, and t stands for time period.

Next, we assumed that R is a linear function of the percentage of total stocks held by institutions, and the ratio of long-term debt to the market value of the firm's common stock. The analysis was based on thirty eight firms in the chemical industry whose shares were actively traded on the national and/or regional stock exchanges. Data were collected from the Standard and Poor's Stock Guide and cover the period 1962-1972.

We tested the equation (R_t) with the intra-firm data as well as the inter-firm data. With respect to the intra-firm analysis, statistical fit was significant (at 5% level of significance) only for three firms. Furthermore, only four firms from the sample of thirty eight enterprises showed a statistically positive relationship between the consolidation of stockholding (as defined by our proxy) and the owners' gains in wealth. The results for the remaining thirty four enterprises suggested no such relationship. The coefficient a_2 was negative for thirty firms. The inter-firm analysis produced similar results. Statistical fit was significant only for the year 1971. The model was also tested with one, two and three years lag in rate of return variables and the results were about the same.

The performance of thirty eight firms in the chemical industry over the period 1962-1972 showed no evidence in support of the separation thesis. Indeed, our test suggests that the wealth of stockholders in corporations with dispersed stock ownership is well guarded.[1] Proponents of the separation thesis have ignored the disciplinary power of competitive markets

THE CODETERMINING FIRM

Codetermination means that employees join shareholders on the board of directors of corporate firms and take an active role in decision making. Germany has been a leader in promoting codetermination in the West. While labor participation in the management of business firms is still a relevant issue in private-property, free-market countries in the 1990s, political debate and economic research on codetermination peaked in the late 1970s and early 1980s.

Two major explanations for the introduction of codetermination in Western Europe are the enhancement of industrial policy and the reduction of worker alienation. The concept of industrial policy dates back to the beginning of the industrial age. It has always meant different things to different people in different periods. But the common denominator of industrial policy has never changed: it is a vehicle for labor participation in the management of business firms.

Support for codetermination comes primarily from social engineers, ideologists (mainly neo-Marxists) and European trade unions. Social engineers see codetermination as an opportunity to do what they think is good for others. They see codetermination as a method for bestowing benefits on labor without any detrimental effect

---

[1] In fact, tests of the kind performed here are not really necessary. There is no law in the United States that says that stockholding has to be dispersed. And the dispersed ownership firm have survived competition from less dispersed firms. The market has then ruled that the voluntary dispersion of stockholding is not inefficient. Otherwise the increasing dispersion of stockholding over the last several decades would have to be attributed to irrationality of private investors.

to stockholders.[1] They tout the merits of industrial policy without reference to its costs. For example, Robert Reich's much quoted The Next American Frontier has little to offer in terms of a cost-benefits of industrial policy. Yet, a critical effect of codetermination is that nonspecific resources (such as labor) on the board of directors of corporate firms encourage opportunistic behavior.

Marxists support codetermination because it is a step in attenuating the right of ownership. H. Gintis wrote:

> I would argue that in this historical period [capitalism] only an expansion of the degree of democratic and participatory control that individuals have over their lives is compatible with full personal development, rewarding social activity, the elimination of class, racial, and sexual antagonism, and material equality. The contribution of political democracy to this end is vitiated by the totalitarian organization of production. Only democracy and participation in production--i.e., the replacement of the capitalist class by the working class as the architects of production, and the accountability of managers and technicians to the will of workers--is compatible with equality and full individual development.[2]

European labor leaders are using codetermination as a vehicle for their own economic gains (i.e., by appointing themselves to boards of directors). The extent to which European workers themselves support codetermination is not clear. In 1976, codetermination was defeated in Switzerland, the only country in which the issue has been put to a vote. For better or worse, American labor unions refused to embrace codetermination. The president of the Machinists Union said:

---

[1] Batstone, E. "Industrial Democracy and Worker representation at Board Level: A Review of the European Experience," Industrial Democracy Committee Research Report, London: Her Majesty's Stationery Office, 1976.

[2] Gintis, H. "Welfare Economics and Individual development: A Reply to Talcott Persons," Quarterly Journal of Economics, 89, May 1975, pp. 301-2.

> We have no interest in replacing free enterprise with a Utopian system...And we believe workers can receive a better share of free enterprise at the bargaining table than in board rooms.[1]

Whatever their motives might have been, American labor leaders saved the country from political pressures to implement contractual agreements that wouldn't emerge spontaneously.

The History of Codetermination in Germany

Codetermination in Germany derives its support from the philosophical origins of industrial democracy. As early as 1835, Robert Von Mohl, Wilhelm Roscher and Bruno Hildebrand, all university professors, proposed to create "workers' committees" in business firms. They felt that capitalism had failed to emphasize moral issues. Their proposal was limited to giving labor the right of hearing. The emphasis was on moral appeals to conscience rather than on legal changes.

In 1848 the first elected German parliament met in Frankfurt. Among other issues, the parliament intended to pass legislation that was called Reichgewerbeordnung. This was the first legislative effort in Germany to create representation of workers in business firms.

The law did not pass but an interesting development occurred in subsequent years. Many provisions of this act were voluntarily implemented by a number of firms. The workers and the owners of business firms found it in their self-interest to work out mutually beneficial contractual agreements without resort to the authority of the state (other than to enforce voluntary agreements). The point is that parties to a contract can identify opportunities for exchange, determine their own trade-offs, and negotiate terms of exchange at a lower cost than that at which a third party could possibly do it for

---

[1] Ellenberger, J. "The Realities of Codetermination," AFL-CIO Federationist, October 1977.

them. While law applies equally to all firms, voluntary contracts allow an owner and that owner's workers to identify and exploit opportunities specific to that firm.

This voluntary emergence of contractual agreements within business firms was eventually arrested by the state. Worker committee laws were enacted in Bavaria in 1900 and in Prussia in 1905. These laws began a process of exogenous changes in the employer-employee relationship. Instead of spontaneous development of contractual agreements that could vary from one firm to another in accordance with their own specific problems, the state began to impose a uniform set of rules on all business firms.

In 1920, a works council law was enacted giving workers the right of hearing in social and personnel questions. In 1922, came another law, according to which one or two employees must be seated on supervisory councils (the equivalent of boards of directors) of business firms. This was the first law on codetermination in Germany. The development that had begun in 1848 had eventually led the country to labor participation in the management of business firms.

In 1946, the military government passed the so-called Act 22, reestablishing works councils. In 1951, came the Montan Act on the "Codetermination of Employees on the Supervisory Councils of Enterprises in the Coal Mining, Iron and Steel Producing Industries" and the stage was set for the current phase in the development of codetermination in Germany. The Montan Act of 1951 covers all firms in the mining and the iron and steel industries that employ at least 1,000 workers. The supervisory council (i.e., the board of directors) of a firm in the Montan industry consists of eleven elected members. Stockholders elect five, employees elect five, and the eleventh member is jointly elected by all supervisory board members.

The Works Constitution Acts of 1952 and 1972 stipulate employees' rights at three different levels of the firm. On the personal level each employee is granted the right of information, hearing, and discussion of issues such as working conditions, hiring, firing, and layoffs. At the plant level, the legislation mandates formation of works councils. These are elected by the employees and vary in size. In general, their function is to act as social agents for the employees in their respective plants. On the decision-making level of the firm, the Works Constitution Acts stipulate that in firms employing more than 500 people, one-third of the members of the supervisory council must be labor representatives.

The Codetermination Act of 1976 applies to all business firms that have more than 2,000 employees. The supervisory board has twelve members. Of these twelve, six are representatives of the shareholders and six are representatives of the employees. At least three members representing employees are appointed by labor unions. The chairman of the supervisory council is elected by the shareholders and he holds the deciding vote in case of a deadlock.

Empirical evidence is not consistent with the claim that codetermination bestows benefits on workers without any detrimental effects to stockholders. After the passage of the Montan Act in 1951, many business firms tried to escape the parity representation on the supervisory board through mergers, reorganizations, and other structural changes. Those adjustments made them subject only to the one-third employee representative requirement of the Works Constitution Act. In the parliament, in the courts, and through direct pressures on individual firms, German trade unions fought those attempts by business firms to avoid codetermination. The same trend continued after the enactment of the Codetermination Act of 1976. In that year, the Act applied to about 650 firms. In the early 1980s codetermination covered only about 480 firms. About 120 firms had reduced their labor force below the 2,000 limit, while about 50 firms had changed their corporate charters. Assuming that both the size and contractual forms of those 170 firms reflected efficient decisions, the post-1976 adjustments are a social cost of codetermination.

Codetermination, Transaction Costs and Incentives

These and similar tendencies suggest that codetermination raises the costs of transactions and creates wrong incentives for members of the team. Why?

There is no law in the United States or Germany or anywhere else in the West that says that there shall be no codetermination. We observe a large number of different types of firms in the West. All these firms have emerged through voluntary contractual negotiations and survived competition from other types of firms. Why then should Germany (and some other West European countries) need laws on codetermination? Why has codetermination not emerged voluntarily like the other types of business firms? Indeed, there are cases in which codetermination has emerged voluntarily but it has not happened on any significant scale. Some quasi-codetermination efforts by employees to buy ownership rights in their enterprises (i.e., United Airlines in 1994) seem limited to declining firms and could be a preferred method of accepting wage cuts. Those efforts, as long as they have to prove themselves in competitive markets, are not at issue. The issue is the law mandating codetermination and protecting it from competition.

The fact that the German government had to mandate the codetermining firm and protect it from competition by other types of firms is the best evidence of its inefficiency. Jensen and Meckling wrote:

> Indeed, labor can start, and in rare cases has started firms of its own. Moreover, firms are free to write any kind of contracts they wish with their employees. If they choose to, they can offer no-dismissal no lay-off contracts (tenure at universities). If they choose to, they can establish worker councils and agree not to change production methods without worker approval. *Moreover, employers would establish such practices if the benefits exceeded the costs.* Furthermore, if laborers value the security and "self-realization" which such participatory arrangements afford them at more than their costs to the employer, they are in a position to offer voluntary changes which it will pay the employer to take *...Since those arrangements are [rarely] observed, we infer that workers do*

> *not value the security, management participation, etc. at more than the cost of providing them* [emphasis mine].[1]

German experience with codetermination reveals some problems. For instance, the election procedure takes up to one year at a cost of millions of marks for direct expenses and loss of working hours. Another cost is that the supervisory council consists of two groups: those representing shareholders and those representing employees. The result is that prior to the official meetings of the board separate sessions are held by those two groups to work out their respective positions on important issues facing the board. Thus, discussions in the board room are not free exchanges of thoughts, ideas and judgments but a sort of bargaining between the two sides. A case in point was the decision by Volkswagen to open a plant in the United States. The decision was delayed for over two years by the employees' representatives on the board. There is also the question of a conflict of interests. Management is supposed to give the board full information about the firm, and members of the board are to treat information as confidential. However, those who represent workers feel that their obligation to employees supersedes any other obligation.[2]

In general, codetermination changes the prevailing relationships among shareholders, managers, employees, and labor unions. Consequently, it affects decision-making powers, appropriability of rewards, and the relationship between risk taking and bearing of costs in firms. The laws, then, change the way the game is played. The relevant issue is to look into the effects of codetermination on the allocation and use of resources.

Whatever the facade of words, terms such as "industrial democracy" and "labor participation" are code words for wealth

---

[1] Jensen, M. and Meckling, W. "Rights and Production Functions: An Application to Labor-Managed Firms and Codetermination," Journal of Business, 52, 1979, pp.472-3.

[2] Paul, M. "Germany's Requiring of Workers on Boards Causes Many Problems," Wall Street Journal, December 10, 1979, p. 1.

transfers. For involuntary codetermination[1] restricts individuals' freedom to negotiate the most beneficial organizational forms. Codetermination shifts the responsibility for decisions to members of the team whose assets are not firm-specific. If the shareholders make an investment decision that is successful, the gains are shared with labor. If, on the other hand, the investment decision is not successful, shareholders alone bear the losses. Codetermination thus violates the risk-reward relationship which, in turn, must raise the cost of equity capital.

Codetermination affects incentives to seek the best use for resources. Given the workers' time horizon, which is limited to their expected employment by the firm, the labor-participatory firm has incentives to choose investment alternatives that shift incomes forward and postpone costs. For example, consider two investment alternatives of equal cost. The expected present value of one alternative is $1,000 while the other yields only $750 at a going rate of interest. However, if the returns from the first alternative are expected over a period of 20 years and those of the second over only 5 years, workers have incentives to push management in the direction of choosing the less profitable one. Even in the absence of profit sharing, wage negotiations and subjective perceptions of job security over their time horizon would provide workers with incentives to prefer business decisions that promise larger annual earnings over a limited time period to those policies that maximize the firm's present value.

In a major study on the consequences of codetermination, G. Benelli, C. Loderer and T. Lys[2] found that the nature of contractual relations in the codetermining firm creates following expected tendencies:

---

[1] That is the only type of codetermination discussed here.

[2] Benelli, G., Loderer, C. and Lys, T. "Labor Participation in Corporate Policy Making Decisions: West Germany's Experience with Codetermination," Journal of Business, 60, 1987.

1. Employees will favor equity financing for its residual claim nature: debt competes with the financial claims of labor contracts. Therefore, codetermination should lead to a reduction in leverage

2. Since other fixed financial claims on the firm's cash flows have a negative effect on their wealth, workers will try to limit the growth of the firm's labor force by favoring the adoption of capital-intensive production processes.

3. In choosing among investment opportunities, employees may favor negative net present value projects, as long as those projects decrease the variance of the firm's value sufficiently.

Codetermination: Conflict or Cooperation

Proponents of industrial policy assert that labor participation in the management of business firms would replace conflict with cooperation. They envision an agreement on ends that is impossible to achieve. In the process, proponents of industrial policy fail to address the social consequences of weakening the right of ownership. Going back to our analysis in chapters 6-8, the right of ownership transfers the guidance of production from specific individuals with limited knowledge, such as regulators, planners and bureaucrats, to the competitive process in which the knowledge of all is used to generate an outcome that no group of individuals could achieve or even foresee. In fact, it is market competition that enhances cooperation by allowing individuals continuously to seek and negotiate mutually beneficial contracts.

The fact that codetermination has to be mandated by the government and protected from competition is the best evidence of its inefficiency. That is, codetermination has failed to survive, on a significant scale, in competitive markets for teamwork. An implication is that research on industrial policy including codetermination has to address a number of problems. If labor participation has positive effects on the firm's productivity, why don't we observe the codetermining firm? Why don't shareholders negotiate with employees a contract that would increase their wealth? If labor participation has to be mandated by law, how can we assert that it is a superior method for organizing production? To say that transaction costs of labor-participatory contracts are too high begs a question: Why are transaction costs too high?

Instead of arguing for codetermination and other forms of labor participation on the basis of technical models that have little to do with the real world, those who favor one or another type of industrial policy should seriously address the issue of the effects of nonspecific resources in labor-participatory firms on transaction costs and incentives.

SUGGESTED READING

Alchian, A. and Woodward, S. "Reflections on the Theory of the Firm," Journal of Institutional and Theoretical Economics, 143, 1987

Easterbrook, F. and Fischel, D. The Economic Structure of Corporate Law, Cambridge: Harvard University Press, 1991.

Pejovich, S. The Codetermination Movement in the West, Lexington: D.C. Heath and Company, 1978 (edited volume).

CHAPTER 13

SOCIALIST FIRMS

THE LABOR-MANAGED FIRM

The labor-managed firm is a socialist version of codetermination: labor participation without private property rights. The labor-managed firm has failed to emerge spontaneously on a significant scale. It has also failed to perform successfully whenever and wherever imposed by fiat. An implication is that the value of labor participation to the employees of business firms is less than the costs to their contractual partners of providing it. Simply put, the competitive process has determined that the labor-managed firm is inefficient.

Yet, J. Dreze, E. Meade, J. Svejnar and J. Vanek, among others, have been asserting that the labor-managed firm is or could be an efficient method of organizing production. Thus, they have to explain its observed failures away. For example, J. Prasnikar and J. Svejnar explained the failure of the labor-managed firm in the former Yugoslavia (the only country that has tried this type of firm on a large scale and over long period) as follows:

> The strong influence of the League of Communists, the communist oriented trade unions and the various government authorities suggests that one ought to examine seriously the extent to which the behavior of Yugoslav firms resembles that of a proto-typical socialist enterprise rather than that of a labor-managed firm.[1]

---

[1] Prasnikar,J. and Svejnar, J. "Workers' Participation in Management vs. Social Ownership and Government Policies," Working Paper No 264, Department of Economics, University of Pittsburgh, 1990, p.5

The argument that the party's political monopoly and the size of the bureaucracy are to be blamed for the failure of the labor-managed firm in Yugoslavia ignores transaction costs that are specific to this type of organization: the involuntary labor-managed firm needs political monopoly and the bureaucracy to protect it from competition with other types of teamwork.

The idea of the labor participatory firm is, however, far from dead. It offers too many opportunities for social engineering and satisfies too many ideological preferences to be discarded on account of its poor showing. Some current proposals for privatizing state firms in Russia, Serbia, Slovakia, Slovenia and Poland contain strong elements of labor participation in management.

Property Rights and the Labor-Managed Firm

Like all other types of enterprises, labor-managed firms differ from each other in terms of internal rules and codes of behavior. It is, therefore, necessary to identify the basic bundle of property rights which sets the labor-managed firm apart from other types of business enterprises. Then, economic analysis can address transaction costs and incentives specific to this type of teamwork.

1. The Employees govern the firm. The employees are decision makers in their respective firms. The decision-making structure of the firm can be expected to take into consideration preferences of the median worker.

2. The employees have claims on the firm's cash flows. This right says that the employees of the labor-managed firm are responsible for all the financial and legal obligations of the firm as well as for the allocation of the residual to the wage fund, investment fund, reserve fund, and any other purpose not explicitly forbidden by law.

3. The employees' rights specified under (i) and (ii) are not transferable. The right of ownership in those rights would, in effect,

allow the employees to sell both their right to govern the firm and their residual claims on the expected future cash flows of the firm.The labor-managed firm would then turn into a private ownership firm.

4. The employees' rights specified under (i) and (ii) are contingent on their employment with that firm. A worker's claim on a share of the residual terminates when that worker leaves the firm. To extend beyond that time these nontradable claims on the firm's cash flow, as some proponents have suggested, would be costly to implement and monitor. It would also impose a rising burden on the firm's future costs of production. This specific right makes the employees' time horizon a critical variable in decision making in the labor-managed firm. The time horizon of an employee is usually defined as that employee's expected length of stay with the firm. It is likely to be shorter than that. First, an important implication of the rights specified under (ii) and (iii) is that the employees cannot diversify their portfolio of nontradable claims on the firm's cash flows. This creates incentives for a conservative bias in decisions that have future consequences for the firm. Second, hiring younger workers is likely to shrink the employees' time horizon. A 45-year-old worker has, in general, a shorter time horizon than a 25-year-old employee. However, the former's time horizon with the firm is likely to be longer than that of a younger worker who hopes to move up by moving around.

5. The labor-managed firm has no ownership in its capital assets. The employees determine the use of assets held by the firm; however, they hold nontradable claims on the firm's cash flows only while they work for the firm.

Property rights specified under (i)-(v) above create some negative incentives and positive transaction costs that are responsible for the inefficiency of labor-managed firms. To alleviate those effects, some writers have proposed various immunizing stratagems which either ignore transaction costs specific to the labor-managed economy or tend to privatize labor-managed firms[1], or both.

Incentives and Transaction Costs.

The bundle of property rights in the labor-managed firm creates some specific transaction costs and incentives. The critical effect of those incentives and transaction costs is on investment decisions of labor-managed firms.

Given the bundle of rights that defines the labor-managed firm, the employees can acquire capital assets through a state agency, by renting them from others, by issuing debt claims, and by allocating a part of the residual into the firm's investment fund.

Acquiring capital through a state agency has many "efficiency" implications. It takes an act of faith to assume that the state will be willing to relinquish its control over the assets given to enterprises. The rental option for acquiring capital assets has two major problems. First, a number of intangible productive assets--such as the firm's investment in the distribution system, the design of products, the training of the labor force, and internal "culture"--cannot be rented. Second, the rental of durable productive assets is a costly method of acquiring capital assets. Rental arrangements create high transaction costs for the owner (including the state) to monitor the use of durable assets, reduced incentives for the user to incur the costs of maintaining and guarding those assets properly, and increased incentives for the user to overuse or misuse rented assets.

It then appears that the labor-managed firm's main sources of investable funds are the claims of debt owners and retained earnings. The former are pure financial claims. As for the latter, since the

---

[1] Flakierski, H. The Economic System and Income Redistribution in Yugoslavia. Armonk: M.E. Sharpe, 1989. Of course, trying to improve the efficiency of the labor-managed firm by introducing some elements of private property rights (and holding back on the right to buy and sell claims) begs a question: Why not do even more for the employees by giving them full ownership? Then they could diversify their portfolio of assets, choose their own risk, and transfer resources to more optimistic owners.

employees have no ownership claims on the firm's assets, they cannot have claims on the monies they leave with the firm to purchase new assets. The employees only hold nontradable claims on the firm's return from those assets, and even that for only as long as they stay with the firm. Thus, we have to make a distinction between external and internal financing of investments by the labor-managed firm.

External Financing of Investment by the Labor-Managed Firm.

The sources of external funds could be state loans, bank loans, interfirm borrowing, state grants, and perhaps some other monies. This section concentrates on the effects of bank credit. Other external sources of funds are subject to similar incentives. The relevant issues for analysis of external financing of investment by the labor-managed firm are:

The employees' benefits from investments financed by bank loans. The employees of the labor-managed firm have nontransferable claims on the stream of annual returns (B) from any specific investment (I) made by their firm. This property right creates incentives for the employees to transfer the firm's cash flows from the future to the present. The employees can run down inventories, fail to replace capital assets, underinvest in the maintenance of capital goods, vote themselves large pensions with no funding provisions, grant themselves large severance payments, sell long-term bonds with no sinking-fund provisions, and so on. To alleviate the effects of those incentives, the government has to invest resources in creating, maintaining, and enforcing a number of constraints on the property and contracting rights of the employees. Examples are the depreciation rules for capital assets, the rules for maintaining and repairing physical assets, the rules for severance payments, and so on. An important consequence of these constraints is that they require a costly bureaucracy (high transaction costs) that is specific to the labor-managed firm.

Implications of the employees' nontradable claims on the firm's cash flows are twofold. First, the employees do not view equivalent present value projects as being equal--those projects with returns that occur more quickly are preferred to those with even flows, and the latter are preferred to investments with yields bunched in later periods. Second, the absence of financial markets means that the rate of interest does not express the present prices of capital goods relative to their current costs of production; it merely measures a cost of investment.

An employee's benefits from any specific investment (I) are limited to the annual returns (B) from that investment over the employee's expected stay with the firm (t).[1] The time horizon of the median member of the collective or whatever the decision-making group happens to be is then a critical factor in choosing investment projects in the labor-managed firm. In comparison, the time horizon of an investor in the private property, free-market economy is irrelevant because the flow of benefits over the productive life of the assets is available to that worker in one lump sum.

The employees' costs from investments financed by bank loans. The employees' costs of any specific investment (I) financed by bank credit is the series of payments (C) to the bank over the time horizon (t). Given the rate of interest, the firm's annual payments depend on the length of time over which the loan has to be repaid (n). The length of the bank loan is a *negotiable* item in the contract between the borrower and the lender. It is thus important to identify the borrower's and the lender's incentives with respect to (n).

Suppose the labor-managed firm secures an investment loan that has to be paid back over a period of time (n). If the time horizon of the firm's employees (t) were equal to or greater than the length of that loan (n), the current group of workers would bear the entire cost

---

[1] The employee's benefits could also be expressed in terms of their present values. We focus on annual returns and costs. It is a simpler approach that has no effect on our results.

of the investment (I). However, if the employees' time horizon fell short of the length of loan, part of the total cost of the investment (I) would be shifted to the next generation of workers in the same firm.

The employees of the labor-managed firm, then, have incentives to seek investment loans with as lengthy a repayment schedule as the banks are willing to go along with. Most preferably, they have incentives to negotiate agreements to pay only interest on investment loans over the current employees' time horizon.

The employees' annual costs of any specific investment (I) financed by bank credit are then

$$C = I\frac{i(1+i)^n}{(1+i)^n - 1}$$

where (n) is the length of bank loan.

The Choice of Investment Projects by Labor-Managed Firms. The employees' benefits from an investment project are the expected returns (B) over their time horizon. The employees' costs from that same investment are the annual payments to the bank (C) over their time horizon. The investment decision of the labor-managed firm depends on the relationship between these two flows. To simplify discussion, we assume that both flows are uniform over the employees' time horizon. Uneven flows would generate different solutions but they would not change incentives. Since the length of loan (n) is determined *contractually* between the lender and the borrower of investment funds, it is possible to adjust (n) so that

$$B = I\frac{i(1+i)^n}{(1+i)^n-1}$$

This equality shows the minimum (n*) required to make a specific investment project acceptable to the employees of the labor-managed firm. The investment decision of the firm, then, depends on the ability of its manager to negotiate a loan that, at the minimum, has to be repaid over a period of time that makes the flow of returns from an investment equal to its production costs times the flow of income over (n*) years from $1 now.

Hence, the length of bank credit (n) is a critical variable in the labor-managed firm's choice of investments.

This result is contrary to the views of Meade, Vanek and other proponents of the labor-managed firm, who argue that the market rate of interest is a critical variable that assures the system of the efficiency of externally financed investments.[1] The difference between the two sets of results arises from these scholars' failure to adjust their models for transaction costs and incentives specific to the labor-managed firm.[2]

The Effects of Changes in the Length of Bank Credit. Suppose that the employees of a labor-managed firm are considering an asset that costs $1,000,000, has a productive life of 15 years, and promises to yield $118,326 per year over a period of 15 years. At the market rate of interest of 10 percent, the present value of that asset is $900,000, and the investment is clearly inefficient. However, suppose that the manager of the firm is able to borrow $1,000,000 from the bank on a 20-year loan at 10 percent. A private-ownership firm would still turn the project down, but the labor-managed firm would not. The employees' annual payments to the bank would be $117,460 per year, while their annual benefits are $118,326. As long as the employees' time horizon is 15 years or less, they would have $866 every year to divide among themselves. Thus they have incentives to make an inefficient investment. The cost shifted to the next generation of

---

[1] Meade, J. "The Labor-Managed Firm in Conditions of Imperfect Competition," Economic Journal 84, 1974; Vanek, J. The Labor-Managed Economy, Ithaca: Cornell University Press, 1977.

[2] In comparison, the decision makers' time horizon and the length of bank loan play no role in the choice of investment projects in the private-property, free-market economy.

workers, including current employees whose time horizon exceeds 15 years, is $117,460 per year over the last five years of the contract.

If the length of the loan is 19.57 years, the firm's *annual* payments (C) to the bank would be equal to *annual* returns (B) from that investment. However, a 20-year loan gives the employees an additional $866 per year over their time horizon with the firm.

An implication is that the manager of the firm has incentives to offer some people at the bank the equivalent of up to $866 per year in cash or specific goods (free travel, a new TV, etc.) in exchange for a 20-year loan at the market rate of interest.

Table 13-1. Relation between the length of loan and rewards offered

Length of loan in years	Benefits (B) in $$	Costs (C) in $$	Benefits minus Costs
19.56	118,326	118,326	-0-
20	118,326	117,460	866
21	118,326	115,624	2,702
22	118,326	114,005	4,321
23	118,326	112,572	5,754
24	118,326	111,300	7,026
25	118,326	110,168	8,158

And the manager would offer even better rewards for longer loans. Table 13-1 shows how changes in the length of loan increase the amount of money the manager can offer in exchange for a "lengthy" contract.

Suppose the time horizon of the employees is 10 years, and the firm has three investment projects under consideration. The productive life of each project and their respective annual streams of benefits per $1 are shown in Table 13-2, columns 1 and 2. Column

3 shows the minimum length of bank loan (n*) that makes the annual flow of benefits equal to the employees' annual cost of those investments. At a 10 percent rate of interest, a private-ownership firm would clearly turn down all three projects because the present value of each project at the 10 percent rate of interest is 90 cents. However, if the manager of the firm were able to negotiate loans in excess of the critical rate of (n*) years, the employees would find all three investments acceptable.

Table 13-2. Property rights and the investment decision

Life of Asset in years	Benefit (B) in $$	Minimum Length of Loan (n*)
10	.146	12.12
15	.118	19.73
20	.106	30.13

A consequence of incentives and transaction costs specific to the labor-managed firm, then, is that *the minimum length of bank credit n* (or any other financial claim) in relation to the employees' time horizon becomes the critical variable for the choice of investments.* Emphasizing the importance of institutions on incentives and transaction costs, Jensen and Meckling wrote:

> Ignoring the agency costs of alternative contractual forms in comparing two systems where the only difference between the two is the contractual form allowed is unlikely to shed light on the major issues. But Dreze, as well as most other writing on the topic, does exactly this.[1]

---

[1] Jensen, M. and Meckling, W. "Rights and Production Functions: An Application to Labor-Managed Firms and Codetermination," Journal of Business, 52, 1979, p. 480

The employees of the labor-managed firm have incentives to negotiate bank loans in excess of their time horizon. One way of arguing for a longer repayment schedule is to exaggerate the life expectancy of assets to be purchased by loans. And when the length of bank credit exceeds the employees' time horizon, the labor-managed firm has incentives to undertake inefficient investment projects such as those in Table 13-2.[1]

On the other hand, the absence of tradeable claims in financial markets must increase the lender's information costs about both the productivity and the life expectancy of assets to be financed by loans, relative to such information costs in private-property, free-market economies. The issue is then whether the lender has incentives to incur those costs in order to negotiate contracts that would equalize the length of loans with the life of assets to be purchased with those loans.[2] There are many possible types of lending institutions, such as private-ownership banks,[3] labor-managed banks[4], various financial institutions, government agencies, and even the so-called super bank.[5]

---

[1] When the employees' time horizon is greater than the productive life of assets, the relationship between (t) and (n) still determines whether an inefficient investment is chosen.

[2] Even if that were the case, such contracts would not eliminate inefficient investments. For that to happen, the time horizon of the employees of the labor-managed firm has to be longer than the expected life of assets.

[3] Given the absence of tradeable claims in financial markets, it is difficult to envision the flow of private funds into labor-managed firms.

[4] Labor-managed banks have yet to happen voluntarily. And if they did emerge spontaneously, the employees' incentives would be for safe loans at the market rate of interest over their time horizon plus whatever "profit-sharing" agreements with the borrower could bring in exchange for longer repayment schedules.

[5] The super bank was invented by Vanek as a government agency which was to make the labor-managed economy efficient by allocating resources to competing firms at prices (interest rates) that clear the market. Like Lange some decades ago, Vanek argued the case for socialism by ignoring the effects of institutions on incentives and

The fact that the labor-managed firm has not emerged on a significant scale in private-property, free-market economies is evidence that the market for business organizations considers the length of bank credit to be greater than the employees' time horizon, and the lender's incentives and transaction costs insufficient to offset the employees' incentives to seek loans in excess of their time horizon.

Internal Financing of Investment by the Labor-Managed Firm.

The employees' non-tradeable claims on the firm's cash flows create two wealth-increasing options for them. The employees can take the firm's residual out as wages and invest in assets such as savings accounts they would own. The employees can also leave a part of the residual with the firm (i.e., take less out as current wages) for investment in new capital assets in which they would hold nontradable claims contingent on employment by the firm.[1]

The employees have the right of ownership in savings accounts (or other owned-assets). They can trade those assets, give them away, will them to heirs, or do anything else with them that is not explicitly forbidden by law. On the other hand, the employees have only nontradable claims on the returns from assets held by the firm. They have claims on neither the assets that their sacrifice of current wages

---

transaction costs, a typical case of a mechanical application of neoclassical economics to an alien environment. What are the applicant's incentives to tell the truth about the expected life of its capital goods? What are the incentives of the super bank employees'? Do they have incentives to find out the expected life of assets the bank is supposed to finance? What is the cost to the bank's superior of making sure that investment funds are allocated at market clearing prices? What are the costs of preventing super bank employees from approving longer loans and sharing the resulting profits with the borrower?

[1] Implications of those differences were researched in detail by Pejovich, S. "The Firm, Monetary Policy and Property Rights,' Western Economic Journal, 7, 1969, Jensen, M. and Meckling, W. "Rights and Production Functions," Journal of Business 52,1979, and a series of papers by Eirik Furubotn and Svetozar Pejovich.

made possible nor the year-to-year returns from those assets once they leave the firm. The employees' cost of any specific investment (I) financed from the firm's residual is the sum total on annuities (y) they could have received over the period (t) by taking the amount equal to (I) out as income and saving their respective shares at the going rate of interest (i). Such an annuity for one dollar is

$$y = \frac{i(1 + i)^t}{(1 + i)^t - 1}$$

The employees' benefits from the same investment (I) financed from the firm's residual is the flow of returns (B) over their time horizon (t). For the employees to be indifferent between internally financed investments and their own individual savings, the former must earn the rate of return (r*) equal to (y); that is, the required rate of return (r*) must be equal to the annuity from one dollar at the rate (i) over the employees' time horizon (t).[1] The rate of return (r*) is then the rate of interest (i) adjusted for the incentive effects of property rights in the labor-managed firm:

$$r* = \frac{i(1 + i)^t}{(1 + i)^t - 1}$$

The rate of return that would make the employees indifferent between investments that are internally financed and their own private investments could be easily calculated. At a 10 percent interest rate and time horizons of 5, 10 and 15 years, (r*) is 26 percent, 16 percent and 13 percent respectively. Also, as in the case of externally financed investments, equivalent-return projects which pay off quickly would be favored relative to those for which payoffs occur further in

[1] Simplifying the assumption that the two investments are alike with respect to risk level and liquidity could only favor private savings.

the future. Once again, incentives and transaction costs apply that are specific to the prevailing property rights in the labor-managed firm.[1]

THE CENTRALLY-PLANNED FIRM

The centrally planned firm in the former USSR and other East European countries was a real folly of the system. Yet, that kind of teamwork played a critical role in the socialist experiment and some of its incentives are present in state-owned firms elsewhere. The basic bundle of rights that defined the Soviet firm were:

1. The manager was the main link between the firm and the planning bureaucracy.

2. The firm's approved production function specified its output quota and the quantities of most variable inputs to be received by the firm, and the plan designated the suppliers of those inputs.

3. The firm had a financial plan which was the monetary equivalent of its production plan.[2]

4. The firm performance was evaluated on the basis of achievement of the gross output target and realization of the average planned costs and planned profits.

---

[1] It is important to understand that the purpose of analysis here is not to demonstrate the inefficiency of the labor-managed firm. The market for the types of business firms has done that. The analysis here tries to explain why the labor-managed firm is inefficient. Also, the analysis applies only to labor-managed firms imposed by fiat and protected from competition by other firms.

[2] State-owned enterprises in the United States also have their budgets determined by a government agency. However, they can use the allocated funds to buy supplies in open markets.

5. The firm was free to hire labor services, but the production plan determined the size of the wage fund. Also, money wages for different skills and levels of education were set administratively.

6. The government allocated new capital goods to enterprises, and transferred the existing ones from one enterprise to another. The firm paid no rent on capital goods in its possession. Thus, the firm bore no cost for having "too much" capital.

The prevailing property rights in the firm suggested a pattern of behavior for its manager. Since the manager's tenure on the job, promotions, and monetary bonuses depended on ability to deliver at least the planned production quota, output played a critical role in the manager's decision making. The production target assigned to a firm made its manager eager to accumulate both fixed assets and variable inputs; for only such accumulation could assure the manager of survival in case of production difficulties, late deliveries of supplies, or other crises. The mechanics of accumulating variable inputs was simple: the manager had incentives to convince the planning bureaucracy that the firm's production function had less efficiency that it actually possessed.

The Soviet manager then had incentives to behave as if his/her utility function were as follows:

$$U_t = f(q_t, S_t : Q_t)$$

where (q) was the output of the firm per period (t) and the parameter (Q) was the firm's planned output quota for period (t). (S) was a measure of the stock of inventory of a specific variable input accumulated by the manager over time and held back from active use in period (t).[1]

The rationale for (S) in the manager's utility function rested on the existence of uncertainty in the Soviet-type economy. Since

---

[1] To simplify discussion we assume that the state does not change the quantity of capital in the firm's possession during the period (t).

input allocations are frequently delivered late or not at all, or with wrong specifications, the firm's possession of unplanned reserves served to help the manager to survive production problems. While managers who failed to fulfill their production plans could have justified a shortfall to the state, they were able to do more for themselves by producing the required output on schedule, whatever it took. Reserves of inputs enabled a manager to meet output quotas even when planned resource allocations were not received. The greater the deficiency anticipated between official input allocations and actual deliveries, the more weight the manager was likely to place on the stock variable (S). We can define (S_t) as the expected delivery of (S) in period (t) plus the previously accumulated stock of this input minus its current use. In practice, the manager could not possibly expect to accumulate inventories of all desired inputs and had to rely on "informal" channels to trade surplus items with other managers.

Because of the absence of open markets for goods and services as well as for financial claims, the planning bureaucracy had high transaction costs in acquiring information about the firm's true production function. The manager's security was thus enhanced by convincing the state that the firm had a lower technical efficiency than was the case. That is, the manager would report the firm's production function as

$$q_t = f(v_t; K_0, m)$$

while the true production function was

$$q_t = f(v_t; K_0, n)$$

where (q) is the flow of output per period (t), (v) is the variable input flow, (K_0) is the stock of capital that has been given to the firm by the state, and (m) and (n) are technical parameters. The difference between the two production functions is that (n) is greater than (m).

The Soviet manager controlled the gap between the two functions by falsifying the true production capabilities of the firm.

However, there were definite limitations on the extent to which the manager could misinform government authorities. A significant departure from the average industry norm would have aroused the government's suspicion. Also, the manager had to be careful in choosing close associates.[1]

In short, the Soviet manager had to reach a decision about the production function to report to the state on the basis of personal willingness to take risks, knowledge of the true production function, and a subjective estimate of transaction costs to the state. Then, given the state's transaction costs and the manager's incentives, the manager was able to create for himself a set of unplanned opportunity choices. The origin of this set lay in the difference between the firm's approved and its true production functions.

The approved production function determined the firm's output quota and its allocation of inputs. Then, given the true production function, the manager could choose to produce no more than the output quota and to accumulate stocks of variable inputs for future emergencies. In that case, the manager would forgo the possible rewards to be had by using extra supplies to overfulfill the production quota. Or the manager could choose to overfulfill the production quota, in that case trading for current monetary rewards future security from accumulating stocks of variable inputs. One more possible choice would be to use some extra inputs to produce additional output and save some for future emergencies.

Contrary to the intent of the government, Soviet managers were able to secure for themselves a set of discretionary choices. And the managers' ability to *create and preserve* that range of choices was key to their survival.

The ability of a manager to accumulate reserves was limited to those supplies actually received and storable (i.e., labor, screws, etc.). Suppose the manager of a firm needs only two inputs, X and Z.

---

[1] It was a risky business for any top officer of the firm to try to replace the manager by informing the state about his lying and cheating. An informer would not only have to face the same problem but would have raised his costs of dealing with other managers.

On the basis of the approved production function, the plan has allocated to the firm 100 units of X and 100 units of Z. Given the true production function, the manager needs only 80 units of X and 70 units of Z to produce the output quota. But what if the firm receives less than 70 units of Z? The manager could eventually explain the production shortfall to the authorities. However, that manager's incentives are to make the state happy, which means producing at least the planned output quota. Hence the manager views the reserves of supplies in another way. In addition to providing security against future shortcomings in the planning system, the unreported stocks are also a source of current purchasing power. Managers could and did trade those stocks with other managers for inputs they wanted, in so-called informal markets. True, the cost of information about exchange opportunities was high and the extent of exchange less than it would have been if managers could have used money. Yet, trade did happen and, most interestingly, it was thanks to these informal markets for supplies that resources moved toward the uses as defined by the plan.[1]

Sooner or later, the manager had to increase the firm's output over and above the production quota. Managers had two reasons for doing this. First, an excess of output over and above the firm's production quota gave the manager a monetary bonus as well as improved standing with superiors (i.e., possibility of moving up). Second, no firm could have accumulated supplies for too long without running a risk of getting caught.

However, overfulfillment of the quota was not a free good. Each time the manager produced more than was expected given the allocation of inputs, the state would revise the firm's production function for the next planning period, expecting the manager to produce more output with the same supply of inputs. An implication of this revision in the production function was a reduction in the manager's set of opportunity choices. Eventually, the firm's true and

---

[1] That is probably why the state tolerated this sort of informal trade between managers. Some went to jail for doing too much, though.

approved production functions would converge. And that would threaten the manager's survival.

As long as managers perceived that their survival depended on the existence of this discretionary range of choices, they had to be eager to find ways to preserve it. In practice this meant that each Soviet manager had incentives to raise each firm's total product schedule by way of improving (n) in the firm's true production as long as managers were able to *conceal* the shift from the state[1] and *choose* the rate at which those improvements were made known to the state. Incentives like these helped the manager to survive by staving off the convergence of the approved and true production functions of firms in the former USSR. Their unintended consequence was to help the economy as well. Incentives to improve technology of production--admittedly strange incentives, but incentives nonetheless--did exist in the Soviet economy. The evidence that those incentives existed is that after so many decades of planning, the Soviet manager was still able to trade current output for additional reserves of variable inputs.

SUGGESTED READING

Furubotn, E. and Pejovich, S.(eds.) The Economics of Property Rights, Cambridge: Ballinger, 1974, chapters 14-18.

Ioffe, O. and Maggs, P. The Soviet Economic System , A Legal Analysis, Boulder: Westview Press, 1987.

Pejovich, S. "Why Has the Labor-Managed Firm Failed?" Cato Journal, 12, 1992.

[1] And that limited both the flow as well as types of innovations in the Soviet economy.

Index of Names

International Studies in Economics and Econometrics

1. T. Harder: *Introduction to Mathematical Models in Market and Opinion Research.* With Practical Applications, Computing Procedures, and Estimates of Computing Requirements. Translated from German. 1969 ISBN 90-277-0096-6
2. A.R.G. Heesterman: *Forecasting Models for National Economic Planning.* 2nd rev. and ext. ed. 1972 ISBN 90-277-0224-1
3. A.R.G. Heesterman: *Allocation Models and Their Use in Economic Planning.* 1971 ISBN 90-277-0182-2
4. M. Durdağ: *Some Problems of Development Financing.* A Case Study of the Turkish First Five-Year Plan (1963-1967). 1973 ISBN 90-277-0267-5
5. J.M. Blin: *Patterns and Configurations in Economic Science.* 1973 ISBN 90-277-0203-7
6. A.H.Q.M. Merkies: *Selection of Models by Forecasting Intervals.* Translated from Dutch. 1973 ISBN 90-277-0342-6
7. H.C. Bos, M. Sanders and C. Secchi: *Private Foreign Investment in Developing Countries.* A Quantitative Study on the Evaluation of the Macro-Economic Effects. 1974 ISBN Hb 90-277-0410-4; Pb 90-277-0439-2
8. R. Frisch: *Economic Planning Studies.* A Collection of Essays. Selected, introduced and edited by Frank Long, with a Preface by Jan Tinbergen. 1976 ISBN Hb 90-277-0245-4; Pb 90-277-1194-1
9. K.L. Gupta and M. A. Islam: *Foreign Capital, Savings and Growth.* An International Cross-Section Study. 1983 ISBN 90-277-1449-5
10. C.A. van Bochove: *Imports and Economic Growth.* 1982 ISBN 90-247-3052-X
11. O. Bjerkholt and E. Offerdal (eds.): *Macroeconomic Prospects for a Small Oil Exporting Country.* 1985 ISBN 90-247-3183-6
12. D. Weiserbs (ed.): *Industrial Investment in Europe.* Economic Theory and Measurement. 1985 ISBN 90-247-3270-0
13. J.-M. Graf von der Schulenburg and G. Skogh (eds.): *Law and Economics & The Economics of Legal Regulation.* 1986 ISBN 90-247-3377-4
14. S. Pejovich (ed.): *Socialism: Institutional, Philosophical and Economic Issues.* 1987 ISBN 90-247-3487-8
15. R. Heijmans and H. Neudecker (eds.): *The Practice of Econometrics.* Studies on Demand, Forecasting, Money and Income. In Honor of Jan Salomon Cramer. 1987 ISBN 90-247-3502-5
16. A. Steinherr and D. Weiserbs (eds.): *Employment and Growth.* Issues for the 1980s. In Honor of Albert Kervyn de Lettenhove. 1987 ISBN 90-247-3514-9
17. M.J. Holler (ed.): *The Logic of Multiparty Systems.* 1987 ISBN 90-247-3515-7

18. J.M. van Brabant: *Regional Price Formation in Eastern Europe.* Theory and Practice of Trade Pricing. 1987 ISBN 90-247-3540-8
See also below under Volume 23
19. A.M. Wesselman: *The Population-Sample Decomposition Method.* A Distribution-Free Estimation Technique for Minimum Distance Parameters. 1987 ISBN 90-247-3603-X
20. P. Coffey (ed.): *Main Economic Policy Areas of the EEC - Toward 1992.* The Challenge to the Community's Economic Policies when the 'Real' Common Market is Created by the End of 1992. 3rd rev.ed., 1990 ISBN 0-7923-0810-7
21. A. Breton, G. Galeotti, P. Salmon and R. Wintrobe (eds.): *The Competitive State.* Villa Colombella Papers on Competitive Politics. 1991 ISBN 0-7923-0835-2
22. S. Pejovich: *The Economics of Property Rights.* Towards a Theory of Comparative Systems. 1990 ISBN 0-7923-0878-6
23. J.M. van Brabant: *Remaking Eastern Europe.* On the Political Economy of Transition. 1990 ISBN 0-7923-0955-3
24. J.M. van Brabant: *Privatizing Eastern Europe.* The Role of Markets and Ownership in the Transition. 1992 ISBN 0-7923-1861-7
25. J.M. van Brabant: *Integrating Eastern Europe into the Global Economy.* Convertibility through a Payments Union. 1991 ISBN 0-7923-1352-6
26. G.W. Kołodko, D. Gotz-Kozierkiewicz and E. Skrzeszewska-Paczek: *Hyperinflation and Stabilization in Postsocialist Economies.* 1992 ISBN 0-7923-9179-9
27. P. Mihályi: *Socialist Investment Cycles.* Analysis in Retrospect. 1992 ISBN 0-7923-1973-7
28. A. Breton, G. Galeotti, P. Salmon and R. Wintrobe (eds.): *Preferences and Democracy.* Villa Colombella Papers on Competitive Politics. 1993 ISBN 0-7923-9321-X
29. K.Z. Poznanski (ed.): *Stabilization and Privatization in Poland.* An Economic Evaluation of the Shock Therapy Program. 1993 ISBN 0-7923-9341-4
30. P. Coffey (ed.): *Main Economic Policy Areas of the EC-After 1992.* 4th Revised Edition. 1993 ISBN 0-7923-2375-0
31. J.M. van Brabant: *Industrial Policy in Eastern Europe.* Governing the Transition. 1993 ISBN 0-7923-2538-9
32. H.J. Blommestein and B. Steunenberg (eds.): *Government and Markets.* Establishing a Democratic Constitutional Order and a Market Economy in Former Socialist Countries. 1994 ISBN 0-7923-3059-5

International Studies in Economics and Econometrics

33. S. Pejovich: *Economic Analysis of Institutions and Systems*. 1995
ISBN 0-7923-3214-8

KLUWER ACADEMIC PUBLISHERS – DORDRECHT / BOSTON / LONDON

www.ingramcontent.com/pod-product-compliance
Ingram Content Group UK Ltd.
Pitfield, Milton Keynes, MK11 3LW, UK
UKHW020651210926
15297UKWH00010B/139

9789401164849